HOPE

Beyond Disappointment

HOPE
Beyond Disappointment

DISCOVERING *the* JOY *of* LIVING
"UNSTUCK"

DAVE HESS

Text design and typesetting by:

Webbdezyne.com
"Let your light so shine before men..."
Cover design by Karen Webb.

ISBN: 978-1-492348-95-5

For Worldwide Distribution, Printed in the U.S.A.

1 2 3 4 5 6 / 16 15 14 13

Dedication

To Mother and Dad—endless thanks to you for teaching me the sweetness of trusting Jesus.

Acknowledgments

I am deeply grateful to so many people for so many reasons.

To my Sheri. For being the best friend I could ever have. Sharing the journey with you—the laughter, tears, dreams, setbacks and breakthroughs—is an experience beyond words!

To Bethany and Richie, Ben and Naomi, and Brandon and Tara. You bring such amazing joy to my heart (Proverbs 23:25). Soar higher, my dear ones!

To Micah and Abby. You are living proof that being a grandparent is not overrated! I'm looking forward to growing up with you—without ever outgrowing our childlike wonder.

To Debra Benedict, Pat Dupert and Elise Jackson. Your tireless labor of love—with edits, corrections and suggestions—has helped make the message clear. I deeply appreciate your hearts.

To Karen Gierhart. For keeping me on track by finding lost things, picking up dropped things and remembering forgotten things—a huge thank you!

To Karen Webb. For inspiring me to write again and helping step-by-step with all the details. And doing it with your signature creativity and contagious joy.

To my Heavenly Daddy. Belonging to You puts all of life in perspective. Being Yours is the greatest joy I will ever know!

Endorsements

I love this book. The message in these pages is desperately needed in the body of Christ today. As I travel throughout the world and minister week after week, I meet so many who are living in deep disappointment and pain who need to experience true hope. Dave Hess draws from his own real-life experiences and from the scriptures to give us a clear path to getting us unstuck so we can live in the joy of hope again. This book is an amazing gift to us from the Lord. You will not be disappointed.

Larry Kreider
International Director – DOVE International
Author of over 30 books

Hope Beyond Disappointment is one of the most powerfully impacting books I have read in a long time.

It reaches deep into the recesses of one's soul and brings comfort and grace.

There is nothing like it to heal a broken heart.

Cindy Jacobs
Generals International
Author of *Possessing the Gates of the Enemy*

Hope Beyond Disappointment is more than a timely book; it is both vital and urgent. I doubt that there is anything that cripples believers more than does disappointment. Without learning to deal with such issues in life, we will never fully step into our destiny as the people of God. Our ability to walk through disappointment, loss and questions without accusing God determines our capacity to live with hope. Dave Hess takes us through his own courageous journey into a place of victory. The power of his testimony and his wonderful insights are available to all who read this great book.

Bill Johnson
Bethel Church, Redding, CA
Author of *When Heaven Invades Earth*
and *Hosting the Presence*

Dave Hess's book, *Hope Beyond Disappointment*, offers a lifeline to those drowning in a sea of hopelessness and depression. It's a training manual dedicated to transforming our minds so that we can view life through God's eternal perspectives, and bring hope to this desperate and dying planet. This book could be the lighthouse in the midst of your storm that will guide you to the shores of peace. I highly recommend this book to everyone who is going through a storm, or knows someone who is!

Kris Vallotton
Senior Associate Leader,
Bethel Church, Redding, CA
Co-Founder of Bethel School
of Supernatural Ministry
Author of ten books, including
The Supernatural Ways of Royalty
and *Spirit Wars*.

Contents

Introduction

"Hope does not disappoint us,
because God has poured out his love
into our hearts by the Holy Spirit,
whom he has given us."
– Romans 5:5

In 1998 I was healed of Leukemia. The vicious attack on my immune system ended. Jesus won the battle! His healing power and love fully restored me by completing an amazing miracle in my body.

Since that time I've shared my story with many people. I love witnessing the dynamic shift that occurs when testimonies of God's faithfulness are released. Just as a drooping plant scorched by the sun will perk back to life when it receives much-needed water, so hope is restored and expectancy rises wherever this message is heard: Jesus still heals. I know He's working miracles today because we have seen and experienced so many of them since my own healing.

Yet whenever I share my story, there are a few people who catch my eye and touch my heart. They have a certain "look" about them. It's an expression that says, "I want to rejoice with you. I want to believe your story—to have faith that my situation can turn around, too. But it's so hard."

It's the look of disappointment.

"I *had* faith," their hearts say. "I trusted. But nothing turned out the way I thought it would. It's as though my hope was betrayed, and now I'm stuck, unsure if I'll ever escape the despair."

I understand where these friends are coming from, caught in the clash between standing firm in their faith, yet facing difficult realities. I know God heals because I experienced His power moving through my body and cleansing me of a

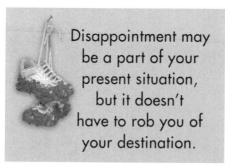

Disappointment may be a part of your present situation, but it doesn't have to rob you of your destination.

vile disease, completely restoring me. I am cancer-free to this day. Yet I've conducted funerals for dear friends who died much too soon, contrary to the prayers we so passionately prayed. I know what the sting of disappointment feels like. It's why I wrote this book.

Disappointment may be a part of your present situation, but it doesn't have to rob you of your destination. Many try to ignore it, but pretending never resolves anything. God loves to help us face reality. The word "truth" as used in the New Testament actually means "reality." When the scriptures say that Jesus is the Way and the Truth, we could translate His name: "the Reality." Similarly the Holy Spirit is the "Spirit of Truth," or the "Spirit of Reality." This core identity of our God is something He wants us to experience in the deepest part of our hearts. The most "real" encounters we will ever have are our encounters with Him.

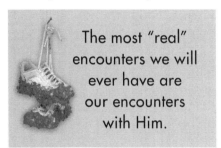

The most "real" encounters we will ever have are our encounters with Him.

He meets us in our darkest places and then leads us into new places. He takes us into realms of His heart where *our* hearts are healed. Our disappointments are addressed. Our pain is put into perspective.

And our hope is restored.

His gift of hope is not only greater than our capacity to reason, it takes us *beyond* our disappointment. You may be so disappointed right now that it seems like the clouds of despair will never go away. You ask, "Will I be stuck here forever?"

There is a way *out* and a way *in*—a way into His very presence. There you'll encounter the greatest joy and peace you could ever conceive. It's so great, it goes *beyond* anything you could ask, think or imagine. In that place, all things are worked together to accomplish His best for you. You are deepened, no longer dampened, by even the most painful events you have ever walked through.

I encourage you to let Him in. Let Him meet you in the place of your disappointment. Receive His restoring love. Receive His gift of renewed hope. Life may disappoint you, but His hope never disappoints.

CHAPTER ONE

The Disappointment Trap

> *"Why, Lord, why have you*
> *brought trouble on this people?"*
> – Moses (Exodus 5:22)

I was stuck.

I hadn't planned to be. Never in a million years did I think I could become so cynical. But like a boa constrictor slowly, stealthily squeezing its prey, setbacks in life had pressed in upon me. In the process, I gave up my joy, lost hope and stopped trusting.

No one event caused it. Lots of things had happened. Some were major, others seemingly minor, but all of them intertwined to become a monstrous web of disappointment.

First, there was a close friend's death after a lengthy battle with cancer. She left behind a husband and two young sons. Then came the passing of a young mother who, after giving birth to her first child, had an allergic reaction to a drug administered during labor. Both events combined to form a strong yet silent current of doubt flowing through my soul. From that point on I began viewing everything through my increasingly negative lens. I had expectations unmet and trusts betrayed.

Constant nagging thoughts rose within me: "How could this happen?" "But we prayed!" "Lord, I thought You promised—and we trusted You!"

And then, the biggest question of all seemed to drown out all the others: "WHY?"

"Why?" It reminded me of my earlier days as a young father, navigating the persistent "Why-daddy-but-why-daddy?" of my children. Now I was hearing the same insatiable cycle inside my own mind—always wanting more information, yet never fully satisfied with the answers. I was stuck and I didn't know how to break out of the "Disappointment Trap."

Disappointment comes in all shapes and sizes. We can be disappointed when others let us down. We can be disappointed with our own failures. But, underneath it all, we can be most disappointed with God.

Especially when He doesn't do *what* we expected Him to do. Or *when* we expected Him to do it.

There is a term used in the Bible to describe being "stuck." David calls it "miry clay" (Psalm 40:2). This expression is a vivid word picture describing a deep pool of sludge. When people plant their feet in this muck, it oozes around their toes, encasing them. When this mud hardens, it becomes like cement. Without outside assistance, someone could be forever stuck in this "miry clay."

Listen to David's joy at being "unstuck":

I waited patiently for the Lord to help me,

and he turned to me and heard my cry.

He lifted me out of the pit of despair,

out of the mud and the mire.

He set my feet on solid ground

and steadied me as I walked along.

He has given me a new song to sing

a hymn of praise to our God.

Many will see what he has done and be amazed.

They will put their trust in the Lord.

(Psalm 40:1-3 NLT)

There is a way out of the "miry clay" of disappointment. Setbacks do not have the power to hold us back forever. Our God is able to remove our "feet" from immobilizing discouragements, restoring us to our journey with Him. He didn't simply do this as a favor for David. He is releasing great waves of His "can-do" grace today—empowering us to break free from the cemented mindsets that are holding us back. He doesn't simply release us from what "was." He sets us free to explore new dimensions of trusting Him, far beyond where we've ever gone before.

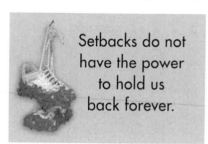

Setbacks do not have the power to hold us back forever.

We are a pioneer generation. We're standing on the shoulders of fiery forerunners who have blazed trails before us. Just as they overcame disappointments in their day, we have the same power available to us to overcome our momentary distresses.

So, let's get started.

CHAPTER TWO

Facing Disappointment

> "We must accept finite
> disappointment, but
> never lose infinite hope."
> – Martin Luther King, Jr.

Disappointment happens. Everyone we meet has been disappointed. And, more than likely, they will be disappointed again. Someone will let them down. A parent. A child. A friend. "Godly" people. Even God Himself.

REALITY CHECK

The first healthy step we can take in getting "unstuck" is to squarely face the reality of our disappointment. Ignoring it won't make it go away. Fantasizing a life free from any difficulties is equally unproductive.

Yet, the opposite approach can be just as deadly — taking the posture of cynicism. Alexander Pope expressed his own pessimistic view of life this way: "Blessed is he who expects nothing, for he shall never be disappointed." What a pitiful way to live!

Life is more than the waiting room for the afterlife. We were made to live life to the fullest. Right now. Jesus calls it "life more than abundantly" (John 10:10) — "more and better life than [you] have ever dreamed of" (MSG). When Paul said, "I want to know Christ *and* the power of His resurrection," (Philippians 3:10) he was not simply referring to being raised up when he died. He was talking about being raised up while he lived. He was describing the power to bring Heaven to him now, declaring that such power allows us to face disappointments without being overcome by them.

Life is more than the waiting room for the afterlife.

Such was the experience of a company of wild worshipers known as "The Sons of Korah." This musical band of praise-hearty men wrote Psalm 42. What I love about the Psalms is the fact that they were written in light of the gritty realities of life. The composers were not strumming harps on a remote, grassy hillside as lambs skipped by, birds sang winsome melodies and flowers swayed in the breeze. Many of them were written in the hard places of life as their authors processed their pain and professed their praise in God's presence. One of the verses of Psalm 42 is a powerful expression of facing disappointment—and getting set free from it:

> *Why are you downcast, O my soul?*
>
> *Why so disquieted within me?*
>
> *Put your hope in God,*
>
> *For I will yet praise Him,*
>
> *My Savior and my God.*

I have no idea what kind of difficulties these men were facing, but they were obviously painful and personal ones. Their honest approach to working through their pain led them into a hope-filled discovery of the heart of God.

ASKING QUESTIONS

Let's take a closer look at some of their words. First, the word "Why?" Asking yourself, "Why?" is an important part of facing your disappointment. It's like looking at yourself in a mirror and saying, *"Wait a minute! Let's stop and take a good look at this! What's going on here? When did this start? If I give in to this discouragement and depression, where is it going to take me? Did it come from God? If not, then why am I putting up with it? If I incorporate being disquieted, discouraged and depressed as my understanding of what 'normal' is, I'll face every day with a 'don't-get-your-hopes-up-and-you-won't-be-disappointed' attitude. Frankly, I am not willing to live like that!"*

The first question asked is, "Why are you so *downcast*?" To be downcast is the same as being depressed. It also describes "sinking down without hope, into despair."

The second question is, "Why are you *so disquieted* (so disturbed or so troubled) within me?" It describes a place of internal rage, fueled by an unresolved offense. When we suppress our frustrations, we may feel that we are concealing our bitterness. But no matter how much we struggle to hold that buoy under water, it will eventually surface and affect us. "Disquieted" involves anything from "a low murmur" to "a constant complaint." It is a "continuous tone of voice," which can even be described as "a murmur or a growl." When we remain "disquieted within," we live with an internal rage. It rages at God. It rages at others. Unless we

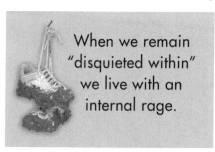

When we remain "disquieted within" we live with an internal rage.

desire to leave this place, even the most encouraging people who want to walk alongside us will find it difficult to help us.

MAKING CHOICES

The Sons of Korah said, "We are not going to accept this as the normal course for our lives! We refuse to keep sinking down into despair. We refuse to keep complaining. No longer will we spurn the encouragement of our friends or pull others into our downward spiral. We choose to call an end to this."

When we believe we've run out of choices, we live like victims. But when we realize that one of

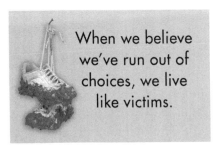

When we believe we've run out of choices, we live like victims.

our greatest God-given abilities is the capacity to make a choice, things begin to turn around. Like Korah's sons, we too can decide: "I will not continue to live a discouraged life. Disappointment will not control me. And so I say, 'No more!'"

Refusing to live disappointed is only part of the equation. The other step is making a choice to "hope in God." As often used in our western culture, hope expresses wishful thinking and a passive expression of desire (i.e., "I *hope* it doesn't rain tomorrow.").

But the Biblical definition of hope is, "the confident and joyful expectation of fulfillment." So the phrase "hope in" refers to "waiting on" or "remaining in a place of trust." To wait on the Lord is not simply watching the time pass, wondering when He's going to do something. It's really not about answering the question, "When?" Waiting on the Lord is about knowing, "Who is with me? Whom can I trust?" When we are waiting well, we are actively deepening that trust. It involves dwelling in His presence, soaking in His love and saying, "Even though I don't see any changes yet, I know You are faithful. You remember Your promises, watching over them until they are fulfilled (Jeremiah 1:12). And I trust You."

And then the final word: "I will still praise You!"

Praise is a decisive action. It's actually an aggressive word meaning "to pick up a rock and throw it; to pick up a javelin and toss it." This Hebrew word, *yada*, describes the thrusting of the hand upward, a prophetic sign of breaking into the heavenly realm, refusing to settle for a mere earthly perspective. Some have said that the raising of hands in worship is the sign of surrender. While we are called to live yielded to God, we are not called to surrender to every circumstance. "I will *yada* You," expressed by an uplifted hand, makes a powerful statement: "I'm not going to live in this disappointed atmosphere; instead, I press through into *Your* atmosphere!"

Sometimes we use the terms "praise" and "thanksgiving" interchangeably. But thanksgiving is what we do *after* the Lord blesses us. Praise expresses our heart

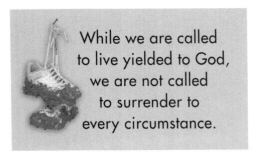

While we are called to live yielded to God, we are not called to surrender to every circumstance.

toward Him, whether the blessing has arrived or not. Praise says, "I will not keep my life in my own hands; I choose to thrust my life into Your hands. Even in the middle of the crazy things that have happened today, I acknowledge this: It may be bigger than me, but it is not bigger than You!"

When Peter said, "Casting all of your cares upon Him, because He cares for you" (1 Peter 5:7 NET), he used an equally aggressive word. Similar to the athletic imagery of *yada, ekballo* means to "throw with great force." It doesn't convey the secretive slip of your request into a prayer box or a passively whispered prayer that you "hope" things will turn out okay. Instead imagine taking the things that weigh us down and forcefully throwing them into the Lord's court. Peter encouraged us to say, "You'll do better with these cares than I will! I was never meant to control, plan and scheme my life. No. I was meant to entrust it to You! So I take my life and shout, 'I trust

You! I trust You!' Worrying about these things won't change them. So I give them to You, confidently believing You are working in ways that far exceed what I can imagine!"

CHAPTER THREE

Expectancy or Expectations?

> *"Expectancy is the atmosphere for miracles."*
> – Edwin Louis Cole

Living in a prolonged state of disappointment is deadly. Mulling over "what should have been," feeding our discontent, and commiserating with other offended people by continually rehearsing our offenses (making one another even more miserable) will all serve to compound the problem. Such choices lead us down a destructive path.

Two of Jesus' closest friends and followers sank into the perplexity of unmet expectations in the days following His death. With their own eyes they had watched Him suffer a horrendous Roman-style execution—crucifixion—and witnessed His lifeless body being placed in a tomb. Reeling from the tail-spin of dashed hopes, they simply wanted to forget it all and put it behind them, completely unaware of the fact that Jesus had risen from the dead.

Picture this: Jesus meets these two dejected friends as they're walking on the road to Emmaus. Literally and figuratively, they have turned their backs on Jerusalem, the place where Jesus, their hope, had been crucified. In sharp contrast to their glumness, Jesus—fresh from winning the battle of the ages—joins them. Victory is all over Him. He has just crushed every force of hell and broken the power of sin, dealing with it at the root. According to Isaiah 53, Jesus not only carried our transgressions to the cross (the sins we have actually committed), but He also cleansed our iniquities (the root cause of our sin). He went right to the core of our separation from God and conquered it. He also conquered the devil himself, every demon, every sickness and every sorrow that would ever plague our minds and our emotions. Imagine His eagerness to share the head-line of the ages with His followers!

Living in a prolonged state of disappointment is deadly.

Don't imagine this Emmaus road interaction as mere small talk among strangers. These two were close friends of Jesus, disciples who had heard His heart and chosen to follow Him. Luke records the fact that they were "downcast" (the same word used by the Sons of Korah in Psalm 42). Their dialogue went something like this:

JESUS: *What's up, guys?*

DISCIPLES: (Shocked) *What do you mean, 'What's up?' Where have you been?*

JESUS: (A sly grin forming on the corner of His lips, as if to say, "If you only knew where I've been. And what I've done for you!") *What have I missed? Tell me.*

DISCIPLES: (Shooting Him a "what planet are you from?" look, one of them agrees to answer this stranger's question) *We're sad about Jesus. Actually, we're disappointed with Jesus.*

JESUS: *Who's Jesus?*

DISCIPLES: *You've got to be kidding! Jesus of Nazareth. He <u>was</u> a prophet. He had His day, but ultimately failed. He preached and promised new life and freedom. We trusted He meant freedom from Rome, and thought by this time He would have liberated Israel. But instead we watched Him die like a common criminal, and all our hopes died with Him.*

EXPECTANCY OR EXPECTATIONS?

Here's the problem with disappointment: it puts expectations on God. And there is a huge difference between <u>expectations</u> and <u>expectancy</u>. Expectancy says, "I trust You to fulfill everything You've promised." Expectations say, "This is *what* I'm expecting You to do, *how* I think You ought to do it, and *when* I believe the best time is for it to happen!"

The disciples' expectation of Jesus was that He would overthrow the oppressive Roman government and set Israel free to be an independent nation once again. But their plans were miniscule compared to what Jesus actually did: instead of supplanting a human empire, He overthrew hell itself! Though

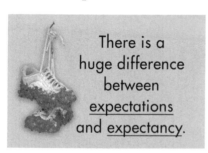

There is a huge difference between <u>expectations</u> and <u>expectancy</u>.

Caesar remained on the throne, Jesus had conquered the devil, death, and the grave, the power of sin and sickness, and every curse and demonic attack! Yet the disciples failed to see and appreciate what Jesus had done because their shortsighted expectations weren't met. They even failed to see Jesus, Himself!

Luke said, "They were *kept from* recognizing Him" (Luke 24:16). The word "kept" doesn't infer that Jesus was withholding anything from them. It actually means that something inside of them (i.e., disappointment) kept them from recognizing Jesus.

EXPECTANCY'S PERSPECTIVE

Jesus wants to break the power of disappointment off us, too, because it clouds our vision and hinders our ability to "recognize" Him for who He really is! When

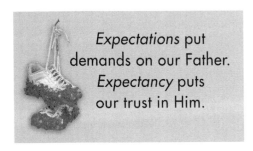

Expectations put demands on our Father. *Expectancy* puts our trust in Him.

our focus is on our frustration, we fail to see Him. The truth is, when He doesn't do things quite like we thought He should, there's a very good reason. He's up to something better! The results may not happen *how* or *when* we think they should, but when the fullness of time comes, His best far exceeds our imagination and misplaced expectations.

This is an urgent truth, one we must hold dear in our hearts, for this is an urgent hour. It's crucial for us to stand firm and not cave in to disappointment's oppression. Things get darkest just before the dawn. Weeping lasts for a moment, just before the joyful break of the new day. Our God is not limping along, biding His time and waiting for the whole planet to crash so He can call it a day. No, He is busy conquering every enemy that plagues the world and leading us in His triumph!

Expectations put demands on our Father. *Expectancy* puts our trust in Him. Expectancy thrives at the core of our relationship with Him. We were created to live expectantly, not cynically. In Romans 5:5, Paul tells us, "He gives us hope that *does not disappoint*." Our Father gives us a "confident expectancy of fulfillment" that, in the long haul, will not disappoint us! Paul continues, *"At just the right time, Jesus died for us."* At just the right time! Our Father is incapable of being either early or late. It would contradict His purposefulness and perfection.

The important question to ask is, *"Who* is with me?" When we ask, *"Why* is this happening?" and other incessant "why?" questions, it results in cynicism and unbelief. Simply put, we will not have all of our "why?" questions answered this side of eternity. As our friend Bill Johnson says so well: "Learn to live with mystery." In the middle of one of my "why-but-why-but-why?" tantrums—attacking the Lord like a band of news-hungry reporters—He stopped me, leaned down and said with a gentle grin, *"Don't demand an explanation for every unmet expectation."*

I've discovered the joy and freedom of declaring this great answer to many of my "why?" questions: "I don't know." It's liberating. Take a moment right now and say it a few times. "I don't know." Try saying it s-l-o-w-l-y. You may feel like the pressure to control your situation lifts from your shoulders. It's okay for us to say, "I don't know. I don't understand." Adam chose the Tree of Knowledge instead of the Tree of Life—the Tree of "Know-It-All" instead of the Tree of "Depend-on-God-for-All." He chose information over intimacy, a rebellion in his heart that said, "Just give me the facts, and I'll take it from here!" But our need is not for more facts; we need His life! In this "Information Age" cyber data is barraging us from every angle, at every minute. Yet the information increase has not brought the transformation the world needs. Peter said it so well, "Jesus, why would we leave You and look for someone else? You alone have the words of life. When You speak, our hearts come alive!" (my paraphrase of John 6:68-69).

Don't demand an *explanation* for every unmet *expectation*.

LIVING BEYOND THE MOMENT

Let this truth settle upon you: Your present situation is not your final destination.

As "Yogi" Berra, catcher for the New York Yankees, says, "It ain't over 'til it's over!" Isaiah said,

"Forget the former things and don't dwell on the past" (Isaiah 43:18). Why shouldn't we dwell on the past? Because God is doing a *new* thing. He says, "Now it will spring forth" (Isaiah 43:19 NAS).

The phrase "spring forth" paints a meaningful picture, describing a plant sending down deep roots. Once the root system is established, it suddenly shoots up with new life at an unimaginable rate. It's like the growth of a bamboo plant, which for the first five years develops miles and miles of roots. Though no growth is visible above the ground, a solid foundation is being established.

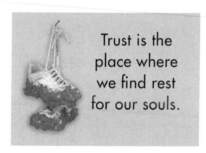

Trust is the place where we find rest for our souls.

Then in the sixth year the plant springs forth, growing two-and-a-half feet per day. Within six weeks, the plant is 90 feet tall. In Jesus' parable of the sower, He describes a plant that springs up quickly, only to whither and die in hard times, due to the lack of mature rooting (Matthew 13:21). In contrast, God's "new thing" will be sustainable and attainable because it's firmly rooted and grounded in *Him*.

When God promises, "I'm going to make a roadway in the wilderness," He means more than creating a narrow path, allowing us to "just squeeze by." "Wilderness" refers to a place deemed uninhabitable.

Yet the Lord says, "I can transform even those places people have rejected—where no one can survive—and make them thriving cities of provision and progress." "Roadway" speaks of the intricate highways developed around cities. It describes the connection and interaction that cause relationships to thrive. We make progress as communication lines are opened. As our hearts are uncluttered by the debris of unhealed disappointments, we begin to truly hear and connect with others' hearts.

God promises us rivers in the desert. Our most devastated places can spring to life again! He pours living waters right on the blighted areas where our dreams died and our confidence was shaken. He seeks out the places of shame where we find it hard to forgive ourselves, putting His finger on them. Where we harbor painful offenses mired in bitterness, and where we've struggled to let go of disappointments with others—right *there* is where His river wants to flow, empowering us to move with Him in fresh vitality. He is calling us closer, and He's calling us deeper. He is restoring our capacity to believe Him once again. He's leading us into deeper places where, beyond simply believing Him, we come to *trust Him.*

A TRUST-FILLED HEART

Trust is the place where we find rest for our souls. It's the exchange in which we surrender our lives into

His hands and receive the power to let go of the disappointments. It's where we rely on Him to carry the things we were never created to carry. We were made to live in childlike trust. "Trust in the Lord with *all* your heart" (Proverbs 3:5) is more than a command. It's a promise that our whole heart has the capacity to be filled with trust.

Trusting Him with all our hearts is a place of simplicity. It's where we learn to quiet our soul and relinquish responsibility for things too difficult for us. We find rest for our souls when we relax in the Lord like a weaned child resting against her mother (Psalm 131). When a nursing baby is hungry, you know it! But when a child is weaned, the "feed me!" cry is replaced with the "hold me!" plea. No longer wanting something *from* her mother, she now wants to share moments *with* her mother.

This supernatural rest—the result of being released from the tyranny of disappointment into the delight of His closeness—is not simply for our benefit. God helps us so we can help others, too. Many people live like orphans, estranged from the heart of their Father. But He is releasing a mighty army of compassionate fathers and mothers, who are setting people free by revealing His fervent love. They value people as the Father values them, seeing them through His eyes. This is what Jesus had on His heart when He told us to pray, "Thy Kingdom come." He longs for the world to experience the same atmosphere He lives in.

For this to happen, it is crucial for us to be unstuck. We cannot afford to be limited in the miry clay any longer—paralyzed by disappointments, offenses and discouragement. He wants us to experience His amazing peace and His fullness of joy. But He doesn't simply want us to *have* peace and joy, He wants us to *bring* His peace and *release* His joy to every relationship we build!

CHAPTER FOUR

I Just Want to Celebrate

"One minute of sincere gratitude can wash away a lifetime's disappointments."
– Silvia Hartmann

Have you ever felt like the perfect storm converged upon the sea of your life, and you were tossed about like a fishing boat hanging vertically on a 150-foot wave, ready to capsize? Does it seem as if circumstances conspired to make you miserable? If so, you are not alone. There are lots of people in the same boat.

In fact, you're never alone. Someone else is always with you.

King David was no stranger to danger. Though honored by God, who called David "a man after My own heart," others hated David. They hunted him, harassed him and sought to end his life.

Out of all of David's psalms, number 34 best captures the intensity of such stressful moments. This song wasn't composed in the afterglow of a worship conference; it was actually written as David reflected on one of his worst days. The Philistines had captured him and he was being held prisoner by Abimelech, the king of Gath, one of the five city-states of Philistia. Why is this significant? Gath was the birthplace and hometown of Goliath. And the Philistines were still furious about this underdog's victory over their champion warrior, in which David killed him with a simple stone and removed his head.

But they weren't the only ones angry with David. At the time they caught him it seemed as if everyone was chasing David. Israel's jealous King Saul was trying to kill him. David's own friends had abandoned him, and his wife thought he was a fool. David was feeling like one of the most isolated people on the planet.

I can only imagine what the Philistines did when they had David "the giant killer" in their clutches. I'm sure they beat him, taunted him and hurled every insult they could conjure. It must have been an unthinkable nightmare. Some translations include this introduction to Psalm 34: a "psalm of David. When he pretended to be insane before Abimelech, who drove him away, and he left." David resorted to feigning insanity in order to escape certain death at the hands of his enemies. He rolled on the ground, growled at them and drooled onto his beard. His antics must have been bizarre, to turn their hatred to pity! Finally they said, "This guy is so weird, we don't want him around!" And they let him go.

As David walked, or ran, away from this horrendous experience, he wrote a song! After one of the most humiliating moments in his life, he made a decision, "I refuse to live the rest of my life outside of God's rest. And I will not let the pain of that disappointing moment govern my life from this point on!"

Listen to the first few lines of his song, "I will bless the Lord at *all* times" (not just sometimes or in the good times—but at *all* times), His praise will always (continually, without interruption) be on my lips. My soul will boast in the Lord. Let the afflicted (those walking through their own disappointing moments) hear and rejoice. Glorify the Lord with me, and let us exalt His name together! I sought the Lord. He answered me. And He delivered me from *all* my fears! Those who *look to Him* (those who consider Him, ponder Him, fix their

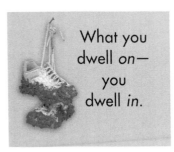

What you dwell *on*— you dwell *in*.

gaze on Him and don't look away) are radiant. Their faces are *never covered with shame*" (v. 1-5).

David uses some powerful words to describe his heart's posture toward the Lord. He passes on to us this life-changing principle: What you dwell *on* — you dwell *in*.

LIVING IN HIS SHADOW

Psalm 91 has been a source of comfort to many people. The promise of living "in the shadow of the Almighty" (v. 1) is an amazing assurance! We get to live protected in His presence! But there's a responsibility *we* have to take for this to be a reality. To dwell "in His shadow" speaks of closeness. The closest place to be with someone is to live in his or her shadow. Yet *we* must make that choice. No counselor can counsel you there. No intercessor can pray you into that proximity. No, *we* must *choose* to place our heart in His presence. As 1 John 3:19 says, we can "set our hearts at rest in His presence."

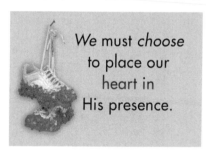

We must *choose* to place our heart in His presence.

David discovered he had the power to *choose*. His unswerving choice was to say, "In my most disappointing moments, I position my heart toward You,

Lord. I will bless You. I will adore You. I will kneel before You to honor You. I will *not* engage in ceaseless hours of morbid introspection, meditating on what has happened to me. I will not allow my circumstances to overshadow me. *You* will overshadow me! I acknowledge today that I am not a victim. I am Yours! I will not surrender my life to depression or yield my life to disappointment. And I will not live as a slave to my emotions or a servant of my situations."

But David didn't stop there. He went on to declare, "Not only will I *not* highlight my disappointment, I'll take matters one giant step forward—I will boast about You! I will praise You!" He literally was saying, "I will *halal* you." This Hebrew term *halal* is the root of the word "Hallelujah." It means "to rave about; to celebrate with abandon; to express joy to such an extent, others may see it as foolish." It is pure, unbridled celebration of the One you love.

It's called "making His face shine upon us" (Numbers 6:25). As a grandfather, I love when this happens with my grandchildren. When I smile at them, I am "lifting up my countenance" upon them. My eyes and my facial expression convey, "You are such a delight, and your life is precious to me. Your Pop-pop's heart is filled with incredible love for you!" When they respond, when their countenance lights up as they smile back at me, I have *made my face shine on their face*. And it thrills me, because they *got* it! They *received* it! They captured a revelation of my heart toward them!

And that is what *our* praise does to *God's* heart! He loves it when our hearts are enveloped in His, and our thoughts are captivated with His thoughts.

MAGNIFYING AND MINIMIZING

David sang, *"Magnify the Lord with me!"* (Psalm 34:3). When we magnify something, we minimize something else. When we worry and complain, we magnify our circumstance, thereby minimizing His presence with us. When we "magnify the Lord" and "exalt His name together," we minimize even our most difficult moments. You see, we can't exaggerate God! We can try, but He's always going to be "more than"

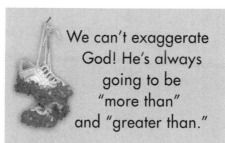

We can't exaggerate God! He's always going to be "more than" and "greater than."

and "greater than." His ways are "past our finding out" (Romans 11:33). His peace "passes our understanding" (Philippians 4:7). He shines "brighter than the sun" (Acts 26:13). He is able to do exceedingly and abundantly far beyond all we can ask or think (Ephesians 3:20). He is eternally greater than and bigger than every passing situation. Circumstances come to pass. But He's here to stay! "He's right there with you. He won't let you down; He won't leave you." (Deuteronomy 31:6 MSG).

David then sang, *"And let's bless and exalt His name together"* (Psalm 34:3). To be honest, the whole concept of "blessing the Lord" used to puzzle me. I was settled in understanding our need for *His* blessing,

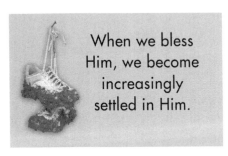

When we bless Him, we become increasingly settled in Him.

but God needing *our* blessing seemed strange. Does He struggle with moments of insecurity? Does He need us to remind Him of His identity? I've come to the firm conclusion that God is eternally secure in Who He is. He doesn't need our blessing. Instead, *we* need to bless Him. When we bless the Lord with all that is within us—we join in the revelation of who He is. This revelation is forever settled in the heavenly realm, but when we bless Him, we become increasingly settled in Him.

THE BLESSING OF BLESSING HIM

As we live this lifestyle of blessing Him at all times, we discover we can never out-bless Him. The moment you start blessing Him, He responds to you. He says, "Do you know what? I'm so glad you're

My son; I'm so glad you're My daughter. I'm thrilled with who you are, and I rejoice over you. I don't hold back in My celebration, but actually dance exuberantly and sing loudly over you (Zephaniah 3:17). I dance the wild celebrative spinning dance of a groom who is elated over his bride (Isaiah 62:5). My delight in you is so passionate, it causes the angels to be mesmerized! They continually study My love for you with great fascination (1 Peter 1:12). Because you have been restored to My family through the blood of My Son, you are cherished in My sight. You are royalty. Seated in heavenly places with Me, you have Throne Room privileges. So, come to Me! My arms are wide open! My heart's wide open! And I reveal My secrets to those who fear Me and draw near to Me (Psalm 25:14). Draw in close and live under My shadow!" *Receive* His invitation. Join our celebrative Father in His party to end all parties!

David continued singing, *"I sought the Lord"* (Psalm 34:4). To seek someone involves making frequent contact. Seeking the Lord means you are in constant connection with Him. He's not your last resort, He's your one and only! And you are purposefully pursuing Him.

The amazing thing about seeking Him is this: He never gets tired of you. He's never had enough of your attention, and you're never too much for Him. You don't wear Him out. He enjoys sharing

His heart with you, and as our Helper, He delights in assisting us to see things from His perspective. Yoked with Jesus, issues are no longer burdensome; they actually become lighter. Your interaction with Him is the highlight of His day! He loves to hear from you and know what's on your heart. In fact, when you can't put things into words, He hears the *cry* of your heart. He's so attentive to you that He even knows how many hairs are on your head (Luke 12:7). He knows your thoughts even before *you* know you are *thinking* them. That's how focused your Father is on you. And *that's* worth celebrating!

CHAPTER FIVE

Greater Than

> *"What we think about God is the*
> *most important thing about us."*
> – A.W.Tozer

I love to read the book of Proverbs. I've been meditating on its wisdom for years. As a young follower of Jesus, I heard Billy Graham say there are 31 chapters in the book. That's a proverb-a-day for most months, with some major proverb cramming on the last day of February! Over the years, I've learned a few interesting things about this fascinating book. Primarily written by Solomon, it captures his desire to prepare his children to think like royalty, poising them to reign during their earthly lives. He wasn't satisfied with seeing them merely get by, take up space or watch the world go by while "sitting on the dock of a bay." He wanted them to change the world, transforming it so the Kingdom of God invades the kingdoms of this world. One time Solomon said to them, "*You will* stand before kings" (Proverbs 22:29). Not you "might," but you "will!" The Lord desires for us to have a noble influence, but that necessitates our learning to think like royalty.

The recurring theme of Proverbs is "wisdom." Wisdom is much more than the capacity to retain information (i.e., the ability to totally clobber your family in a game of Trivial Pursuit). Rather, the word means "skill in living." It involves knowing how to initiate, respond, interact, process, progress, succeed and thrive. It's freedom from being clueless. Wisdom is the God-given ability to know what to do and the skill to know how to do it. When we're leading a life filled with responsibility and are able to walk appropriately while responding to various circumstances—that's wisdom.

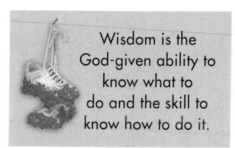

Wisdom is the God-given ability to know what to do and the skill to know how to do it.

OVERCOMING SMALL THINKING

With this in mind, let's examine a piece of a proverb and then put it in context. Proverbs 24:10 states, "If you falter in times of trouble, how small (or how limited) is your strength." Faltering involves "fainting" or "slackening." It means to back off when things become overwhelming. To give up. "To sink" and become "disappointed" and "disheartened." The root of this word conveys, "being reduced, made small, shrinking in your ability to perceive." In essence, faltering is "shrinking thinking." It's seeing yourself as small and insignificant, and perceiving everything else—people's opinions, life's struggles, momentary setbacks, even spiritual attacks—as being much bigger than your ability to navigate them.

The "day of trouble" can also be translated as "adversity." The language of the Old Testament is full of pictures and images, where one Hebrew word often describes a vivid series of events. "Adversity" is such a word. Visualize this: you are trying to maneuver through a narrow passageway with high walls of rock on either side. As you proceed, the trail gets tighter and tighter until your head becomes lodged between the rocks. You're stuck, and it seems like there's no room to turn and no way to escape. That's what a "day of trouble" feels like.

Now, let's put it all together. When we allow the *circumstances* outside us to determine the *climate* inside us, we become immobilized. Our strength is lessened by our limited thinking, not by the tight spot itself. Proverbs 23:7 tells us, "...as [a man] thinks in his heart, so is he" (KJV). Meditating on fearful and anxious thoughts will atrophy our faith. When Moses sent twelve spies into Canaan to scout out the territory, ten returned feeling overwhelmed by what they saw. Walled cities. Giant armies made up of giant warriors. "Forget the colossal grapes, we're outa here! Compared to them, we're mere grasshoppers! They'll squash us under their sandals!" Stacking their perceived abilities next to their supposed obstacles, the spies' "shrinking thinking" evaporated their strength. They chose *their* limited perspective over *His* great promise to "surely" give them the Land (Genesis 50:24).

In the same way, *we* sometimes limit God. The most debilitating kind of small thinking is to view God as "less than" able to help us. Israel repeatedly put God to the test by doubting Him and demanding that He prove Himself.

"Shrinking thinking" limits God!

They "limited" Him (Psalm 78:41) by their lack of faith, loss of trust and diminished expectancy that He would be their "very present help in trouble." When they lost sight of Him, they forfeited their strength in Him. Stuck in *dis*appointment, they lost their clear and powerful discernment and missed *His* appointment. This same attitude filled the hearts of the people of Nazareth, Jesus' hometown. The very Son of God could only do a few miracles there because of their unbelief. "Shrinking thinking" limits God!

TURNING IT AROUND

Of course we want to leave behind our limited understanding and make room for God to move in power! Remember the sons of Korah, the composers of Psalm 42? Overwhelmed with disappointment, they stopped and asked themselves, "Why are we so 'disturbed' inside (Psalm 42:5)?" "Disturbed" also involves being stuck in one place. Stuck in a memory. Stuck in regret. But then the realization hit them: "We have a gift from God called 'hope.' Hope is the ability to confidently expect. We have been putting our hope in the past—in pain, in disappointment. We've simply been expecting more of the same. How futile is that? Let's put our hope in God!"

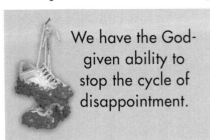

We have the God-given ability to stop the cycle of disappointment.

We have the God-given ability to stop the cycle of disappointment. And we have the God-given authority to turn things around. It's called the "gift of repentance." It includes the power to think new thoughts and see from a new perspective.

Let me be honest: I spent three years of my life stuck in the valley of disappointment. I'm not sure where the expression "pity *party*" originated. I've found that self-pity is anything *but* a celebration. It is a land of distortions, where vain imaginations thrive. And before long every "perpetrator" in your life begins to appear increasingly villainous.

A series of real or perceived "injustices" had led me down a path toward the conclusion that I was a victim. Initially I failed to see—or even dared to consider—my own part in the process. I allowed myself to become disappointed with people. People I had trusted. I wondered: "How could they betray me? Why would they say such demeaning things? And even worse, why would they say them behind my back?"

But then came the painful discovery: I realized I was disappointed with myself. Why had I so quickly rolled over and given up? Why did I struggle with being truly honest and vulnerable—both with other people and myself?

Finally came the most sobering realization of all: I was deeply disappointed with God. Where was He in my time of need? Why didn't He ride in on His great white horse and rescue me? (I know He has one—I read about it in the book of Revelation!) I didn't expect Him to open the earth and swallow my enemies whole. But a little "smiting" might do the trick.

RESPONSE ABILITY

Joyce Meyer has a way of lovingly slapping you in the face and bringing you back to reality. One day her words hit me square, shaking me from my self-imposed prison: "If you complain—you remain. When you praise—you get raised." Through her words, the Father was telling me, "Son, it's time to take responsibility for your life." I was ready to get "unstuck." Like Ebenezer Scrooge having his encounter with the spirit of Christmas future, I caught a glimpse of my potential future...and it was not pretty! I saw myself as a bitter old man, isolated in the corner of a retirement home, telling anyone who dared to listen my tales of woe. Suddenly I realized that if I continued living in dis-appointment, I would forfeit my appointed destiny. It was my choice whether I wanted to pass on a litany of pain or a legacy of hope!

One of my recurring questions in the valley of disappointment was, "But I don't understand! Why did this happen?" My cry for understanding went largely unmet for some time. Then one day this revelation touched my heart: Peter refers to our relationship with Jesus as "the faith" in 2 Peter 1:1. "The faith." He didn't call it "the understanding," but rather a "precious faith"—one we won't always understand. In fact, we weren't created to understand everything. The Lord fashioned our hearts to be completely filled with trust in Him (Proverbs 3:5). We were not made to "lean on" (find our sole stability and support in) the realm of our understanding. Frankly, our understanding is overrated. Even when our *mind* is unable to understand God, our *heart* is fully capable of trusting Him.

"GREATER THAN"

Our capacity to trust in the Lord increases as we shift from seeing Him as "less than" to beholding Him as

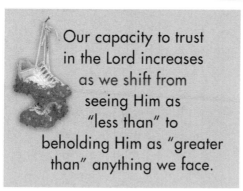

Our capacity to trust in the Lord increases as we shift from seeing Him as "less than" to beholding Him as "greater than" anything we face.

"greater than" anything we face. Jesus' hometown of Nazareth was bound by less than thinking when it came to Jesus. Not only did they refuse to call Him the Son of God or refer to Him as a prophet, they didn't even honor Him as a rabbi. He was known as merely "the carpenter's son."

At one point, Jesus addressed this less than perspective by telling them who He really is (Matthew 12). He began by stating that He is "greater than

Jonah." In fact He said that at the judgment, the people of Ninevah would stand and call Nazareth condemned. *The people of Ninevah* believed Jonah, yet *you* don't believe the One who is *greater than* Jonah.

I'll admit that Jonah is not one of my favorite Bible characters. He was a coward, a racist, and an irritating whiner. When God directs him to go on a mission to Ninevah, he books a cruise in the opposite direction! Jonah's disobedience endangers the entire ship's crew. Jonah's next "brave" move was to commit seaside suicide by volunteering to be thrown overboard. But then God, in His compassion, sends a "great fish" to rescue him from the bottom of the ocean. After he's burped aground on the shore of an isolated desert island, God causes a gourd to grow a large leafy umbrella over Jonah, protecting him from the sun (and sparing his life yet again). When the gourd withers, more whining ensues. Finally Jonah makes his way to Ninevah. He begrudgingly warns them to repent, although his heart is still not aligned with God's redemptive purposes. He then takes a front row seat on the hillside overlooking Ninevah and, box of popcorn in hand, awaits the fireworks of God's judgment to annihilate the city. Much to his chagrin, the entire population repents! Even the animals repent! It's an *amazing* revival. Think about it: Jonah delivered a half-hearted message to a people he didn't care about, and everybody got right with God!

Jesus said, "I'm greater than Jonah." Why? "Because I love. I care. I lay down My life for the whole world! I can transform your life and turn your family around. And your neighborhood. And your city. In fact, I can transform entire nations. Whatever your situation—I can do this!"

Don't you think it's time we see Jesus as "greater" than rather than "less" than? When we believe we are "less" than the circumstances, we're living like victims. And when we believe God is "less" than our situations, we live powerlessly. When we're more in awe of what's happening *around* us than *Who* is *over* us, defeat is inevitable. So let's rest confidently in knowing He is greater than. Always.

Jesus continued His comparisons, declaring, "I am greater than Solomon" (Matthew 12:42). Solomon's wisdom was remarkable. There never had been such a wise, insightful person on the planet. God gave him "a wise and discerning heart" (1 Kings 3:12). The Queen of Sheba and other

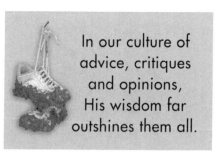

In our culture of advice, critiques and opinions, His wisdom far outshines them all.

leaders traveled from far-off nations to glean from him. More than retaining information, Solomon creatively knew what to do and how to respond in any given moment. God said of Solomon that there has never "been anyone like you, nor will there ever be" (1 Kings 3:12). Yet Jesus has *much greater* wisdom than the wisest man in all of history! He is truly marvelous—One worthy of marveling at. In our culture of advice, critiques and opinions, His wisdom far outshines them all.

Better yet, not only does He have all wisdom, our Father is generous in dispensing it. James, Jesus' half-brother, said, "If any of you lacks wisdom, he should ask God, who gives generously to all" (James 1:5). And His wisdom is timely. Jesus advised us not to worry when we find ourselves in a tight spot, called to task for the One we trust and follow. He encourages us not to worry, "For I will give you the words and wisdom that none of your adversaries will be able to resist or contradict" (Luke 21:15).

It's time for us to search out the wonders of the Lord. We don't have to wait for Heaven to do that. God has secrets He wants to reveal to us now. They're not things He's hiding *from* us, but revelation He's been holding *for* us—appointed moments that unfold in the right season, at times filled with opportunity. Disappointment says, "You believed this before, and look where it got you. Remember the clueless moments, when you had no idea what to do? The times you gave the wrong answers and made foolish choices? Why should tomorrow be any different? Nothing is going to change." But the One *greater* than says, "These are new days. Redemptive days. I can take even your worst moments and work them into the fabric of your life, expanding your perspective and deepening your wisdom. Your past only has power if you allow it to rule today." As Graham Cooke articulates, "It is time to stop living 'present-past' and start living 'present-future.'" It's time to trust the 'God of all hope' to 'fill you with all joy and peace as you trust in Him, so that you may overflow with hope by the power of the Holy Spirit' (Romans 15:13).

It's time to trust the One who is *greater* than. Jesus said His ability to keep us (to guard and guide us) is greater than satan's ability to snatch us (John 10:28). His ability to encourage us is greater than our heart's ability to condemn us (1 John 3:19-20). He is greater than the power of shame—the inability to forgive yourself. And He is much greater than the power of condemnation—making the pronouncement that you will never change. He is so much greater than your heart's capacity to shame you, condemn you and limit you.

Sometimes we face life like Gideon. God spoke to him, calling him a "mighty man." Gideon's response? "You've got the wrong guy!" God replied, "No. You're the man I've called. You can rescue Israel from the oppression of the Midianites. So, 'go in the strength you have and save Israel out of Midian's hand. Am I not sending you?'" (Judges 6:14). Gideon hedges with, "*But* Lord." It's an oxymoron worse than "jumbo shrimp." In effect Gideon was saying, "I have an objection and I oppose your command, O Lord, who reigns with absolute authority in all the universe!" He then offers his reason for resisting God's clear command, "How can I save Israel? My clan is

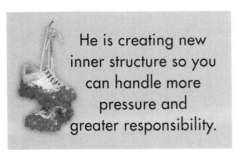

He is creating new inner structure so you can handle more pressure and greater responsibility.

the weakest in Manasseh, and I am the least in my family" (Judges 6:15). In effect, "I'm the weakest link, the worst of the

worst. I'll never amount to anything. And nothing can change that." As long as we view life through the 'less than lens'—less than the circumstances, less than the call, less than the need—we relinquish ourselves to a victim lifestyle.

As long as you think your circumstance is greater than you, you'll be like the person with their head wedged between two rocks. Stuck. But the moment you realize there is a greater than God—who made you a greater than person—you will live unstuck, rising up, walking and conquering the power of disappointment. You do not have to live your life stuck!

You may not even like yourself right now—but God loves you! He may not like some of the things you've been doing, but He loves you. *Trust His love.* Take hold of it in your heart. As you yield your heart to His, the Holy Spirit does a work in you. He informs and instructs, activities involving much more than the exchange of information. When He "informs," He puts a new form inside. When He "instructs," He establishes new structure. He is creating new inner structure so you can handle more pressure and greater responsibility.

It's time to face life from a greater-than vantage point. John informs us, "As He (Jesus) *is* so are we in this world" (1 John 4:17). It doesn't simply mean "as He *was* when He walked the earth," but as He "*is*" right now. He is seated in undisputed majesty in the heavenly realm, with all of His enemies as His footstool. And He, the God of peace, is crushing the enemy underneath *our* feet (Romans 16:20). We are seated with Him in Heavenly places. That's far superior to simply walking with Him along the shores of Galilee, wearing a bathrobe and flip-flops. As He *is*—so *are we*! The same power that raised Him from the dead, broke the power of sin and defeated every demonic foe has also raised you up to boldly live an entirely new life. He's given you power over all principalities and all powers. Greater is He who is *in you* than he who is in the world (the devil). And in Jesus' name, *you* will do "greater works" than Jesus did while *He* walked the earth (John 14:12).

It's time to stop acting like "drama kings and queens" with the devil, panicking and obsessing when we are "under attack." The moment you submit your life to Jesus, you become part of a battle. It's nothing new. It's an age-old battle—the longest-standing conflict in human history. It's not against people, but against "spiritual forces of evil in the heavenly places" (Ephesians 6:12). We "wrestle" them, and wrestling is different from any other type of warfare. It can be close, intense, straining, draining hand-to-hand combat. But think about this: if you have a grip on the enemy, resisting his schemes, and the One "greater than he who is in the world" reigns in your life—who should

If hell had a film channel, *you* would be the horror movie. The enemy is terrified of you.

be afraid? We must stop being terrified and traumatized by the enemy of our soul. God informs us that demons believe and tremble in fear because of Who He is. If hell had a film channel, *you* would be the horror movie. The enemy is terrified of you. Isn't it time we live like the greater-than children we really are?

CHAPTER SIX

Shaking the Dust

*"Twenty years from now you will be more
disappointed by the things that you
didn't do than by the ones you did do.
So throw off the bowlines.
Sail away from the safe harbor.
Catch the trade winds in your sails.
Explore. Dream. Discover."*
– Mark Twain

I can still hear the voice of the Timex watch commercial's narrator, John Cameron Swayze. A Timex wristwatch was strapped to the tread of a bulldozer, and then driven around a construction site. After countless turns and tumbles, the dozer stops in front of the camera, and the watch is removed from the tread and brought close to the lens for the viewer's inspection. As the second hand continues circling with precision inside the dial of the watch, Mr. Swayze's commanding voice would say: "Timex. Takes a licking, and keeps on ticking."

You, too, have been made to take a licking and keep on ticking. In God, you are more durable than you know. Jesus put it this way, "Truly I tell you, among those born of women there has not risen anyone greater than John the Baptist" (Matthew 11:11). That's quite a statement. Jesus is saying, "This is the truth—I'm not just being flattering. No one has ever walked this planet, shaken this planet, and impacted lives on this planet to the extent which John the Baptist has."

GREATER THAN JOHN THE BAPTIST

Then Jesus made this mind-boggling statement, "Yet he who is *least* in the Kingdom of Heaven is *greater* than he" (WEB). What a revelation! The "least" of us will be deemed "greater" than John the Baptist. Understand that the word least does not imply less in value. God doesn't place value judgments on His people. In fact He says it is foolish to make comparisons by ranking or classing ourselves. Rather the word means the "youngest," the spiritual infants. It's describing someone who has just surrendered his or her life to Jesus, receiving a first breath of Holy Spirit oxygen. These are the ones Jesus calls "the least," saying, "Someone just beginning to experience new life in Me—is greater than John the Baptist!"

There are many admirable attributes of this heroic martyr. First of all, he was *unshaken by external pressures.* He described himself as a "reed not shaken by the wind" (Luke 7:24). Neither the religious environment nor the political climate could manipulate him into conformity. From his locust diet to his unconventional camel skin wardrobe, John the Baptist was his own man. His message was powerful and penetrating, yet far from popular. He withstood the pressure to compromise, living true to the convictions God had established in his heart.

Secondly, he was *discerning.* John had the ability to see through religious performances. Often when we read the Gospels, we can tend to see the Pharisees as the bad guys. Yet, in the days of John the Baptist, they were viewed as the most righteous men on earth. Projecting an image of pious spirituality, they were revered far above other worshippers. The word *Pharisee* means "separatist," a title born out of their desire to separate themselves from anything that would contaminate them. In their religious zeal they created extra rules—just to be certain they were keeping the commands of God. For example, to make sure they would "remember the Sabbath day and keep it holy," they added thirty-nine additional laws to the fourth commandment. Eventually their rules became equal to the command itself. In their minds, to truly keep the Sabbath holy, you could not cook a meal, ride an animal, have sexual relations with your spouse or gather food in the fields. The Pharisees not only kept these rules, but also strictly enforced them on others.

John saw the emptiness in such meticulous rule keeping. Because of his love for them and a desire to see them set free, he spoke directly: "I see your outward behavior. On the surface, you appear holy. But deep inside you are a 'brood of vipers.'" He wasn't trying to insult them with the worst phrase he could imagine. He was saying, "What you are breeding is deceptive." A viper never moves in a straight path. You can't pin them down. They squirm away. (Remember the snake on the South Carolina state flag with the phrase "Don't tread on me"?) John discerned, "You breed a viper-like religion. It is dishonest—projecting an image of purity while, deep within, your heart is unchanged. And it is evasive—resisting a vibrant encounter with the living God. I am here to prepare your hearts for His entrance into them. I reveal this to you so that He may release you from religion's deceptive clutches."

Perhaps John's greatest quality was his *ability to confront and transition people into life-changing encounters with Jesus.* He had the power to bring the Pharisees, the most entrenched religious performers, to the place of repentance. There in the wilderness by the Jordan River, some of these self-righteous leaders confessed, "Our ways have not been working. We need to be changed from the inside out. Prepare us to receive the One you are sending." Although not all of the Pharisees received John's ministry, many of these leaders (quite possibly Nicodemus in John 3) had their lives transformed through the ministry of John the Baptist.

Now consider what Jesus says about you. The youngest follower of Jesus is more powerful than John the Baptist. There is an unshakeable tenacity at the core of your being. You can't be sold out, held back, backed down or compromised. You have discernment. You aren't clueless. You are His sheep, and His sheep know His voice. His sheep are not "dumb." You see what's right and what's wrong. You are able to see what God is doing and pour yourself into it. You are empowered, not only to confront dead religion, but also to transition people into living encounters with their heavenly Father through Jesus. They will come to the Father through Him. He has infused all of these qualities into His people. John the Baptist wasn't shaken by the world. He *shook* the world. This same

There is an unshakeable tenacity at the core of your being.

potential resides in you. And we have been called to something even greater. By His grace we can *change* the world!

This is why the issue of being stuck in disappointment must be resolved. There is so much more for us than living as powerless spectators. We are meant to be history makers. World changers. Climate transformers who are bringing His Kingdom to the earth.

Someone may have said to you regarding the region where you live, "I'm discerning a religious spirit here." Guess what? I believe you can say that almost anywhere on the planet, because satan himself

By His grace we can *change* the world!

is a religious spirit. He appears "*as* an angel of light," attempting to deceive people. He goes around "*as* a roaring lion," attempting to intimidate people. But Jesus *is* the Lion of the tribe of Judah. He *is* the "Lord of Hosts, the God of angel armies." He *is* releasing a greater-than work in our hearts, empowering us to combat every religious lie—awakening people to behold Jesus, follow Jesus and live as lovers of Jesus. We have been born for such a time! Our release from the dregs of disappointment is crucial, so we're free to enter into all we've been called to experience and express of His heart.

BEING LIKE KING DAVID

Our circumstances do not have the power to limit us. Listen to this promise: "On that day the Lord will shield those who live in Jerusalem so that the fee-

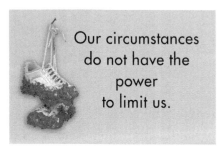

Our circumstances do not have the power to limit us.

blest among them will be like David" (Zechariah 12:8). The word feeble describes those who are shrinking and stumbling. Those who are ready to quit. He says to us, "The time is coming when My people are not only going to be greater than John the Baptist, they are going to be *like* David. Not *act* like or *pretend* to be like—they will actually *be* like David. And nothing they are going through will be able to prevent Me from breaking through."

The promise of being "like David" is extraordinary. David was a man who experienced *unparalleled intimacy with God.* God gave him one of the greatest compliments when He described him as "a man after My own heart." David pursued intimacy with the Lord no matter what was going on around him. One of the recurring themes of David's Psalms is this: whether facing trials or experiencing triumphs, whether feeling abandoned or being celebrated—I will find a place of rest in the heart of God. From a shelter in a storm to a picnic on the battlefield, David discovered that nothing could separate him from the presence of God. He even made this bold confession, "Even if I make my bed in hell, You are there with me!" (Psalm 139:8).

God said, "The feeblest in My Kingdom will be *just like that*!" Those who are ready to quit—overwhelmed by disappointment—will be able to say, "Nothing is going to interrupt my intimacy with God!" His relentless revelation will come to them: "Nothing. Absolutely nothing can separate you from My love. Receive and rely on it. Let My love cast out every fear. Stand with Me, knowing you are fearlessly loved with a never-ending love from an everlasting Father."

Another powerful dynamic of David's life is the way he *influenced others to experience the same intimacy with God he enjoyed.* Rather than keeping it to himself, he led an entire generation into unparalleled closeness to the presence of the Lord.

When David became king, the people of Israel would go to the Tabernacle of Moses to meet with God. In that amazing place His mercy was abundant, sins were cleansed and hearts were made right with the heart of God. The Tabernacle had three parts. The outer court was the place where the people received ministry. In the Holy Place, the priests ministered to the Lord and received His ministry to them. The third part, the Holy of Holies, was only accessed one day each year—on the Day of Atonement. This day was set apart for the high priest to seek cleansing for the sins of the entire nation. The Holy of Holies was the grandest place of them all. It was unlike any other because *the Presence of God* was there. He was *with* them!

Tabernacle simply means a "tent" or a "dwelling place." The symbol of the presence of God in that place was consolidated in a wooden chest, covered with gold, known as the *Ark of the Covenant.* It was a tangible way God conveyed to them, "I am among you. Right beside you. Covering you and protecting you. And I am the *Holy* One—unlike anyone you will ever know."

But King David discovered one major problem with the Tabernacle of Moses. The Ark of the Covenant was missing. It had been taken by the Philistines, not just yesterday, but twenty years prior. Israel had worshipped in the Tabernacle for twenty years— *without the presence of God!* (They were merely "house-sitting" while the Host was not at home!)

David said, "This is unthinkable! No more will we go through the motions of worship without the Presence of God. We're bringing the ark back!" After a series of "good intentions gone bad," David finally returned the ark to Israel. But instead of restoring it to the Holy of Holies compartment of Moses' tabernacle, three miles north of Jerusalem on Mount Gideon, David established a new tabernacle on Mount Zion, just outside of the walls of Jerusalem. Until David's son Solomon built the Temple forty years later, both of these tabernacles were utilized. One *with* the Presence of God, the other *without*.

There were other significant differences between these two tabernacles. Rather than building his dwelling place with three compartments, as Moses had done, David made his entire tabernacle one large Holy of Holies. In Moses' tent, only the high priest could enter the Holy of Holies. But in David's tent, all of the priests could minister before the ark, making a way for all the people to experience the presence of God. Many other positive changes followed. Unlike Moses' tabernacle, David's tabernacle was filled with singing, shouting, clapping and dancing.

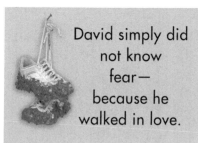
David simply did not know fear—because he walked in love.

New songs were written. Instruments were played. For the next forty years, those who desired to could experience the presence of God twenty-four hours a day, seven days a week. David led an entire generation into uninterrupted intimacy with God.

The overflow of this unparalleled intimacy resulted in *the entire nation experiencing unparalleled authority over their enemies.* One of the things I admire most about David is his fearless heart. He simply did not know fear—because he walked in love. When David saw one of his father's lambs in the jaws of a lion, he boldly approached it. Face to face with a lion,

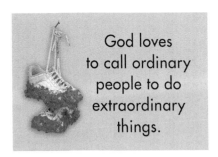

God loves to call ordinary people to do extraordinary things.

he rescued the lamb and killed the ferocious beast. When David saw a giant cursing the name of the Lord and intimidating the army of the Lord, he refused to back down. This same loving tenacity carried over into his ministry as king of Israel. David conquered every enemy attempting to rise up against the people of God. During David's reign "there was peace on all his borders" (1 Kings 4:24). With every enemy nation subdued, Israel experienced the favor of God because of one man's obedience.

Receive the promise of your Father: "Even at your weakest moment—tempted to cave in to disappointment and despair—I will make you *like David.* Nothing will separate you from Me. No strategy of the enemy will overtake you. You will actually inspire others to encounter Me in *their* time of need."

God loves to call ordinary people to do extraordinary things. He said to Noah, "I've got an assignment for you. I'd like you to join Me in this adventure. Let's preserve the whole human race!" This wasn't just, "Hey, let's build a boat." This was an enormous task. But Noah and his family did it! You and I are living proof that Noah succeeded on his mission.

FAITH LIKE ABRAHAM

In a similar way, God gave a word to Abraham.

He said, "Abraham, I am calling you to be a father of nations. I am calling you to be a father of faith—to walk with Me in faith, so generations yet to come will be inspired to trust Me in the same way you do."

Abraham: "You know what?" [snickering a little, under his breath] "I'm going to try to believe that." [working hard to stifle his laughter] "Just one problem. I don't have any kids! In fact," [unable to contain his amusement any longer, breaking out in uncontrolled giggles] "I *can't* have any children. I am past my prime. Lord, you're about ten years too late with Your assignment."

God: "That's no problem for Me. Just say 'Yes' and watch what I can do!"

[After a season of doubt and delirium, Abraham comes to his decision]

Abraham: "Okay. I'll trust You. Your promise staggers me. But I trust You because You don't make promises You can't keep. You are faithful. I don't know how You're going to do it, but I guess that's why it's called 'faith,' not 'understanding.'"

And God fulfilled His promise to Abraham. And to David. And to you, too. Even at your "feeblest" moments, if you trust Him, He will do things that can only be received by faith, not by understanding.

SHAKING OFF THE DUST OF DISAPPOINTMENT

My son Ben is a pilot. I enjoy flying with this man of peace and wisdom. Nothing seems to shake him up. I could hear him saying something like this through the intercom to his passengers on a flight, "May I have your attention please? We seem to have just lost a wing. So, if I could have all passengers at window seats on the left side of the plane stick your arms out the windows and flap—we should be fine. And grab an extra bag of peanuts as the cart goes by."

An aviation friend was talking to me recently about a plane crash in a nearby state. He said, "I think this crash could have been avoided. They didn't take the time between trips to de-ice the plane." The ice and debris from the previous flight kept them from soaring on the next flight—and they collided with a mountain.

What a Kingdom principle! The dust of disappointment from past "flights" can keep us from soaring on the next journey. It's time to "de-ice" our planes. It's time to "shake off the dust" of past disappointments. In Isaiah 52:2 the Lord addresses Israel as she's just coming out of captivity to Babylon. He said, "Shake yourself free from the dust. Rise up, O captive Jerusalem. Loose yourself from the chains around your neck, O captive, My captive daughter of Zion." You are now *My* captives. You're not their captives any longer. Adjust to the new day! The apostle Paul, when held captive by the Romans declared, "I

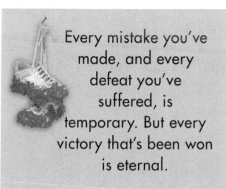

Every mistake you've made, and every defeat you've suffered, is temporary. But every victory that's been won is eternal.

am a prisoner of the Lord Jesus Christ. I'm not *their* prisoner. I'm *His.*"

The Lord has given us all we need to "shake off the dust" of every disappointing experience. Where we've failed, been rejected or dejected. Where people failed us. Or where we believe God failed us. Without "shaking off the dust" we will bring a less-than posture into the next opportunity. We'll back off a little more, and a little more, until we expect nothing to ever change.

Every mistake you've made, and every defeat you've suffered, is temporary. But every victory that's been won is eternal. The defeat came to pass. But the victory brought you to a new place of authority—and it lasts!

Jesus said, "Whoever will not receive you, accept you, welcome you, or listen to your message—leave that house and shake the dust off your feet" (my paraphrase of Matthew 10:14). "Shaking the dust" was not cursing the house. It was saying, "I refuse to bring the disappointment of *this* experience into my next experience."

Some disappointments are not just personally upsetting, but also painful. This is especially true when the loss involves someone we love. King David's son died, and he spent days mourning, weeping until he could no longer cry. Grief is a very genuine expression of love. It's how love processes loss. David processed the tragedy of losing a son, grieving every vanished dream he had held in his heart. But 2 Samuel 12:20 records his next steps: "He washed himself"—shaking off the dust of broken dreams. "He anointed himself"—receiving new grace for a new day. "He changed his clothes"—preparing himself to walk into a new place. Then, "he came into the house of the Lord and worshipped." Later, he returned to his own house and, when he requested, his servants sat food before him and he ate.

You don't have to live like a victim—to even the most traumatic events.

You *can* shake off the dust—and soar again!

CHAPTER SEVEN

Outrageous Joy

"*Joy is the serious business of Heaven.*"
– C.S. Lewis

"*Joy is not necessarily
the absence of suffering,
it is the presence of God.*"
– Sam Storms

"*When we are powerless to do a thing,
it is great joy that we can come
and step inside the ability of Jesus.*"
– Corrie ten Boom

There we stood, poised for action. Just around the corner and down a few steps was "Christmas wonderland," our present paradise. For weeks we had folded the corners of pages in the Sears & Roebuck catalog, circling the exact toys we wanted. Now, we could almost see them. They awaited us beneath the tree. No longer in a magazine—they had materialized in our house.

The night before we hardly slept. At the first sign of the new day, one of us would wake the others. Excitement pumping through our veins, we took turns checking on mother and dad to see how long they would hibernate. Until, finally, there was a sign

We were never made to live without hope.

of life. Dad's nose twitched. And one eye opened. In unison we would shout, "It's Christmas!" The approval to descend upon the wrapped treasures seemed to take forever. I can still feel that moment of child-like anticipation. The "my-heart-is-in-my-throat-I-think-I-just-might-wet-myself" expectancy that leaps in the soul of a hope-filled child.

FILLED WITH HOPE

We were never made to live without hope. To live without hope is to be "most miserable." Hope is more than wishful thinking. The biblical use of "hope" describes the joyfully exuberant expectancy of fulfillment. It's like kids at Christmas, just before they see the gifts. True hope is truly joyful. And it's confident, too.

Paul prayed this prayer for his friends, *"May the God of hope fill you with all joy and peace as you trust in him, so that you may overflow with hope by the power of the Holy Spirit*" (Romans 15:13). When we invite Jesus into our lives, He comes not just to help us survive. He moves in to cause us to thrive and enjoy life at a "more than abundant" level. He is the One who "daily loads us with blessings" (Psalm 16:18). The One who blesses us with "every spiritual blessing" available "in the heavenly realm" is utterly amazing! He is worth our endless adoration.

Life has disappointments, yet we don't have to be victimized by them. Remember the sons of Korah in Psalm 42? We may be disappointed, but we do not have to become disquieted—sinking down into hopelessness.

REFUSING HOPELESSNESS

The apostle Paul was no stranger to disappointment. In fact, in 2 Corinthians 11 he includes a whole list of frustrations in his life, "I was beaten so many times I lost track. I was thrown in prison countless times as well. I was struck with the Roman whip—thirty-nine lashes, three times. I was stoned and left for dead. Then I was shipwrecked three times as well, once spending a day and a night in the ocean (with the theme from the movie *Jaws* playing in my head). False friends betrayed me, and almost everywhere I went I faced trouble." Paul then concludes his list by referring to something even more troubling to him. You see, in the writing style of his day, when you made a list, the last item mentioned was the most important. Paul was saying, in effect, "More than being shipwrecked and beaten and stoned and betrayed, there was a daily issue I constantly faced, 'the daily pressure of my concern for all the churches'" (2 Corinthians 11:28).

The word *concern* or *burden* refers to "things not yet realized" or "things not yet fulfilled." Paul was conveying, "I know what it feels like to be bombarded each day regarding things yet to become reality. Yet, I have learned how to resist caving in to disappointment. I have discovered how to avoid living disheartened."

Paul shares his discovery quite clearly in his letter to his friends in Philippi. For Paul this breakthrough into resisting hopelessness was more than a theory;

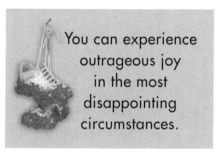

You can experience outrageous joy in the most disappointing circumstances.

he thoroughly "road tested" this truth. Actually, he wrote his letter to the Philippians while in prison. A Roman prison. Far from the standard American prison with game rooms, weight rooms, shower stalls and mattresses. This was a pit—a hole in the ground that allowed barely enough room to move and breath. The Romans were not known for their hospitality.

The theme of his letter could be summed up in this phrase, "You can experience outrageous joy in the most disappointing circumstances." Deplorable surroundings do not have the authority to deplete your gladness. The condition does not have the power to condition you!

At the heart of this letter Paul says, *"Rejoice in the Lord always. I will say it again: Rejoice!* [Such an important issue, he mentions rejoicing twice.] *Let your gentleness be evident to all. The Lord is near.* [Literally, so devoted to you, He never plans to leave you.] *Do not be anxious about anything, but in everything, by prayer and petition, with thanksgiving, present your requests to God. And the peace of God, which transcends all understanding, will guard your hearts and your minds in Christ Jesus"* (Philippians 4:4-7). These are words of wisdom from a wise father who knows what it means to be disappointed. Let's take a little time to ponder them.

PAUL'S REMEDY FOR DISAPPOINTMENT

One of his primary words to us is, *"Dwell in the presence of the Lord."* Who you abide in is more important than *what* you are going through. Stay in, live in, and abide in the presence of the Lord. The nature of the Lord is that He is "near." David said, *"We praise You, O God, for Your name is near"* (Psalm 75:1).

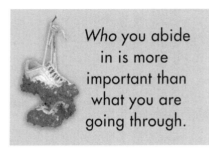

Who you abide in is more important than what you are going through.

The name of the Lord is more than His title, it's His identity—who He is deep inside. The very nature of the Lord is to be near you. He *wants* to be near you. In fact David said, "I could never escape Your presence, even if I tried" (see Psalm 139:7-12).

The real issue is not, "Is the Lord with us?" The important question is, "Are we with Him?" Are we longing for and receptive to His presence? While Jacob slept, his dreams became permeated with Heaven, as the Lord sought to reveal Himself. The heavens opened, angels ascended and descended, all glory erupted around him—and Jacob slept through it. When he awoke he said, "Surely the Lord was in this place *and I did not know it!*"

You can almost feel the longing in Jesus' heart as He sat with a Samaritan woman by a well one day. She failed to see Him as He was, oblivious to His identity. At one point He said to her, "If you only knew who I really am. I'm a gift to you from God. You came here for water, but I could give you 'living water.' I can bring you into a life that is continually refreshed in the presence of God. All you need to do is ask" (my paraphrase of John 4:10). There is "fullness of joy" we experience as we become increasingly aware of His presence with us. This brings us to another word from Paul.

Saying it twice for emphasis, Paul admonishes us to, *"Rejoice."* Rejoicing does not mean, "trying to be happy, pretending to be elated, forcing a laugh or pasting on a smile." Its meaning carries us into much deeper places than we could ever manufacture. It conveys this thought, "to be well and thrive in the company of another." It is not feigned or rehearsed. It is an honest response to someone who brings joy to your heart. It's not about pretending; it's about "being with." Really being "present to the Lord."

Why do we omit being present to the Lord? It's usually because we are either fretting about some-thing that has happened, regretting the past or we are dreading the future. Whatever the case, we miss the moment we are in, along with all of the opportunities available to us right now.

That's why Jesus said, "Don't worry about any-thing." That's why He specifically said, "Don't worry about tomorrow." Why? "Because today has enough issues that require your full attention. And I will give you all the grace you need. Immediate grace for your immediate needs. I'm not pouring out tomorrow's grace today. I'm not giving daily bread for tomorrow—only for *today*. I am *for* you. I am all you need in this moment."

The word rejoice has a "right now" sense to it. Rejoicing in the Lord involves being present to Him *now*. Disappointment says, "I'll be happy *when*...I'll be so glad *when*...." Disappointment relegates everything to another time. It places a condition on our

Rejoicing in the Lord involves being present to Him *now*.

ability to find joy. Disappointment confuses happiness with joy. Happiness is based on what is *happening*. But joy is unconditional. It's all-terrain. Because rejoicing in the Lord declares, "Right here. Right now, I'm with You, Lord. Most importantly, You are with me. And You will never leave me. I can thrive in Your presence while things are thrashing around me. You are faithful. And You will take me through."

Disappointments can seem ominous. They can even feel eternal, as if to say, "You will never be able to move beyond this moment." This is why it is vital for us to walk in Father's perspective. In His eyes, problems are "momentary light afflictions" (2 Corinthians 4:17). In our eyes, trials only wear us out.

But from God's perspective, they are building us up and filling us with His glory. He calls it "an eternal weight of glory." He designed us to face life this way, focusing on the eternal weight of His glory, because it is here to stay. Our momentary troubles are coming to pass.

Then Paul continues, *"Don't worry about anything, but pray about everything."* He said, *"Pray at all times."* Even in the anxious moments—pray. Even when you don't feel like praying—pray. In fact, I'm finding the most powerful moments seem to happen when I don't feel like praying. Think about it. When you don't feel like praying, who do you think is trying to keep you from praying? Can you imagine the Holy Spirit saying, "Oh, don't pray now"?

When we pray we are to pray without anxiety. Only with thanksgiving. Prayer and worry are polar opposites. Sometimes what we think is "fervent prayer" is actually fearful prayer. When the disciples asked Jesus to teach them how to pray, He didn't

When we pray we are to pray without anxiety. Only with thanksgiving.

say, "Here's how you do it. Cry out, 'O God, where are You? Why is this happening? I can't take it any more! Don't You even care?' And then you may want to follow up with, 'O please, please, please, please hear me! Please, please do something, I beg You!'" Sometimes when we pray we are more aware of the thing we are asking for—than the One we are spending time with.

Jesus said, "Pray in this way. Our Father, who is in Heaven, Holy is Your name." That statement lays the foundation for prayer. *We* have a Father. He is not just "my" Father. He is "our" Father. We're in this together. He is not removed from us. Though He is "in Heaven," He reigns over the entire heavenly realm. There is none who will ever rival Him for that position, as His throne is established throughout the ages. He will never be removed from the place of ultimate authority over all. And His name is "Holy." He is "other than; set apart." Another way of stating the word "holy" is, "He is in a category all by Himself." He alone is Holy.

I am an earthly father. I dearly love my growing family—my children, their spouses, my grandchildren and all the rest. Through the years, I have made mistakes. There's nothing like family to reveal your "growth areas" and your "immature zones." Yet, I have prayed for and been attentive to their cries. One whimpering cry of, "Daaaaaaddy, there's something in my rooooom," was enough to cause gallons of adrenaline to stream through my bloodstream. Emerging from my sleep like a trained warrior (at least in my head), I would mount the staircase in stealth form, ready to face my foes in the night. If I, as an earthly father, love my children passionately, just imagine what our Heavenly Father who is in a category all by Himself, has in His heart for us! That's why we pray "with thanksgiving."

When you hear the word "thanksgiving," don't simply resign it to the table with a feast on November 25th. Don't limit thanksgiving to the annual exercise of trying to think of "one thing you are thankful for" as you "go around the table," only to get frustrated that your Uncle Ben once again picked your "one thing" two seats before it was your turn! Actually the word "thanksgiving" means, "to live under the influence of another." So when

The purpose of prayer is to connect with Him.

we live the lifestyle of being thankful, He continually influences us. We remain in a place of awe. We have a Father who is over us and over all things. I'm not under my circumstance. I'm not under the people mistreating me. I am under His protection. He rules over this, and He is over all of these things. Just to drive this powerful perspective home, Jesus said, "When you conclude your prayer, declare, 'Yours is the Kingdom. Yours is the power. Yours is the glory forever and ever. So be it!'"

Then Paul said, "As you live in this place of outrageous joy and ceaselessly thankful prayer, you will make a powerful discovery: *Even before the answer comes, His peace will come!*" If we think the only purpose for prayer is to get answers, we are extremely shortsighted. The purpose of prayer is to connect with Him. To discover His heart. To receive His perspective and stand with Him in that place. We "watch and pray" as we are joyfully expectant of receiving revelation. We pray with purpose, thankful for the privilege of co-laboring with Him.

He has the bigger picture. He knows the end from the beginning. So many in Israel wanted Jesus to be their champion Messiah, sent to end Roman oppression. But they were greatly disappointed when He did not respond to their political agenda. Feeling disenchanted, many lost interest and rejected any thought of following Him.

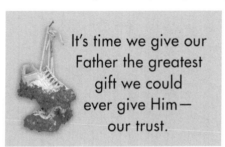

It's time we give our Father the greatest gift we could ever give Him— our trust.

His death at the hands of religious leaders and the Roman regime only reinforced their shattered hopes. Imagine if Jesus had simply done what they desired, bringing them temporary relief from an earthly power, only to forfeit His larger plan—the liberation of the entire human race from the dominion of satan and his demonic horde! How often do we long for our comparatively small desires to be met, bringing momentary fulfillment, while being oblivious to His greater-than purpose accomplishing eternal rewards?

It's time we give our Father the greatest gift we could ever give Him—our trust. Let's rest our lives in His capable hands and trust the One whose ways are higher than ours. Paul says, "When you posture your hearts to rejoice in Him, thankfully coming under His influence, His mighty peace comes and stands guard at the door of your life. He guards your mind from fearful tirades and vain imaginations. He guards your heart, keeping it from failing you." Jesus said, "Men's hearts will fail them because of fear." You don't have to go there. He will guard your heart. He's able to keep you from falling. He's bigger than your heart. Even when your heart tries to condemn you, He's bigger than your heart (1 John 3:20). Immeasureably bigger.

His joy is everlasting!!

CHAPTER EIGHT

A Worry-Free Zone

"Worry is like a rocking chair—
it gives you something to do
but it gets you nowhere!"
– Glenn Turner

"It is not the cares of today,
but the cares of tomorrow
that weigh a man down."
– George MacDonald

As long as we remain stuck in disappointment, we will contaminate our future with worry. Worry is the practice of taking today's disappointments and projecting them onto tomorrow's opportunities.

Disappointment despises what *did* or *didn't* happen. Worry *dreads* what is *about to* happen. Disappointment *dwells on* the worst memories. Worry *anticipates* the worst scenarios.

Nothing can *make* us worry. We *choose* it as a response to life. As my friend Graham Cooke says: "Stress is always an inside job"[1] Worry is the byproduct of seeing our lives from an earthly perspective instead of a heavenly one. While our feet are firmly planted on this planet, we are "seated in heavenly places in Christ" (Ephesians 1:3). We have a new vantage point. We are no longer victims. Our cares do not have the right to consume us.

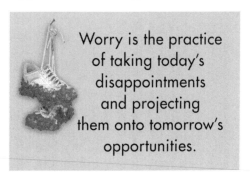

Worry is the practice of taking today's disappointments and projecting them onto tomorrow's opportunities.

THE IMPACT OF WORRY

It's time for us to stop accommodating worry as a normal part of everyday life. Peter said, "Cast all your cares on Him because He cares for you" (1 Peter 5:7). Because this phrase has adorned countless Christian greeting cards and posters, it can become so familiar and soothingly poetic that we fail to receive its radical message. Peter was not a poet. He was a rough and tumble fisherman, a businessman, and an occasional swordsman (with limited proficiency). More than trying to say something profound, he was giving an urgent warning.

The word Peter chose has an interesting history. Before the word "cast" or "cast off" appeared on the pages of our Bibles, it was part of a story familiar to many in Peter's day. It's from a tale of a little boy who was playing outside, oblivious to a deadly snake coiled and ready to strike the unsuspecting lad. According to the story, the boy's father, spying the snake, grabbed it. With one fluid motion the father broke the neck of the reptile and threw it far from his son, securing his safety. *Yay, dad!* The father's response was referred to as "casting"—*the violent removal of something deadly.*

Worry is deadlier than we know. Like the lethal serpent, worry can creep into our thoughts, our words, and eventually permeate the atmosphere of our lives. Jesus warned us about difficult times coming to our planet, saying, "Nations will be in anguish and perplexity" (Luke 21:25). Yet His greatest concern was not about international turmoil, but the way many would respond to challenging days. He warned of "men's hearts failing them for fear" because they will be "apprehensive of what is coming on the world" (Luke 21:26).

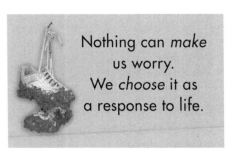

Nothing can *make* us worry. We *choose* it as a response to life.

Worry can paralyze us, poisoning our thoughts with panic. Early editions of *Noah Webster's American Dictionary of the English Language* define panic as "acting like Pan, the god of the underworld, i.e., satan." Because of Jesus' triumph over satan at the Cross, our enemy is terrified. "Even the demons believe [that there is one God]...and they tremble in terror" (James 2:19 NLT). Our adversary knows as long as we trust God, he's defeated. So he works tirelessly to terrify us—to force us to withdraw from the world and into our worried hearts.

CONFRONTING OUR WORRIES

It's for this reason Peter makes his bold appeals, asking us to confront our worries. Do not surrender another moment of your life to care, fear or worry. Get rid of it. Cast it far from you. The same power that raised Jesus from the dead is at work in you. There is no greater power in the entire universe than His resurrection power. He is empowering us to rid our hearts of worry. He's imploring us to be anxious for nothing! Jesus is turning worriers into warriors. He's releasing multitudes of His family from hiding *from* the world to going in*to* the world to change it and heal it.

For some of us, worry has been a familiar spirit—a family trait passed from one generation to the next like a treasured heirloom. Fear can cause people to huddle together, sharing story after story of worrisome woes. This sad form of co-dependent comfort becomes a terrifying "tie that binds." Though captivating and consuming, the generational curse of worry can be broken.

Think about this. Abraham was a liar. One of Abraham's biggest deceptions was telling King

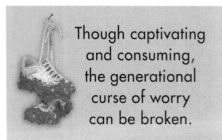

Though captivating and consuming, the generational curse of worry can be broken.

Abimelech of Gerar that his wife Sarah was his sister. Because he believed the king would kill him if he knew she was his spouse, Abraham said, "If you want her you can have her." To save his own neck he was willing to prostitute his wife!

Then look at Isaac, Abraham's son. He spun the same lie in a similar situation. In fact Isaac was in the very same place—the land of Gerar. "When the men of that place asked him about his wife, he said, "She is my sister," because he was afraid to say, "She is my wife." He thought, "The men of this place might kill me on account of Rebekah, because she is beautiful" (Genesis 26:7). The acorn did not fall far from the tree! Yet the perpetuating of this generational legacy of lying did not stop with Isaac. It passed down to the third generation!

Isaac's son, Jacob, was a twin. Even in childbirth Jacob tried to outmaneuver his brother Esau. As Esau descended the birth canal on his way to becoming the firstborn son, Jacob grabbed his brother's heel. His valiant attempt was unsuccessful. Baby Esau emerged into the world with his brother's hand clutching his foot. This action earned Jacob his name, "Heel Grabber." In our vernacular his name translates as a "cheat, conniver, manipulator, con man." How would you like to go through life with a name like that?

Jacob didn't like it either. He desperately wanted this curse to be removed from his life. In Genesis 32:22-31, there is an amazing account of Jacob's face-to-face encounter with God. He had such a powerful time in His presence that Jacob gave a name to that piece of ground. He called it "Peniel"—"the face of God." During his time of wrestling with God, he held fast to Him and said, "I need Your blessing in my life. Bless me. Break this curse off of me." Within moments, God gave Jacob a new name and a fresh start. He changed his name to "Israel"—you have "overcome." You are now a "prince who reigns with God." The generational curse was broken, and a new legacy of "royal overcomers" had just begun.

He will do the same for you. He can change your name from worrier to warrior. From overwhelmed to overcoming. Hold fast to His promises. He's faithful to every one of them. As David said, "I sought the Lord, and He answered me; he delivered me from *all* my fears" (Psalm 34:4). You can "cast *all* your cares upon Him." When He delivers us from *all* our fears, He releases us into a new realm of being anxious for nothing. That's what deliverance is. A package is not *delivered* until it reaches its destination. Your destination is life in a Kingdom where the presence of the King causes you to "fear no evil" because He is with you! Worried about nothing. Praying about everything. Grateful in every situation because you are under the influence of heaven.

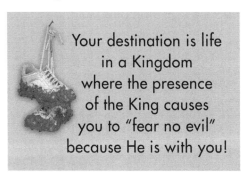

Your destination is life in a Kingdom where the presence of the King causes you to "fear no evil" because He is with you!

THE GREAT EXCHANGE

When we "cast our cares on Him," we give worry an eviction notice. But simply being "worry-free" is not all He has for us. Jesus wants to make an amazing *exchange*, emptying us of worry in order to fill us with praise. Jesus' first recorded sermon was a declaration of Isaiah 61. He announced a season of new beginnings: Jubilee—the year of the Lord's favor. Debts would be cancelled and lost things would be restored.

Among a list of many significant changes, He announced that a garment of praise would replace a spirit of heaviness. The spirit of heaviness is a "dark, subtle cloud that creeps in upon" its victims, causing them to be weighed down with fears, resulting in loss of vision, confusing our ability to discern. The garment God described was more than a coat or cloak. It involved being "enveloped by, completely wrapped in and consumed with" praise. The praise He fills us with is a distinct, brilliant revelation of His heart, resulting in a bold expression of our love for Him. This *halal* praise is a boasting or raving about God, so uninhibited in its expression, it could be misinterpreted as foolish. As we become consumed with Him, worship displaces worry.

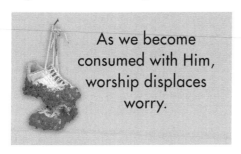

As we become consumed with Him, worship displaces worry.

Paul's solution to worry is simple. "Fill your mind with the thoughts of God." He spelled it out this way in his letter to the Philippians, "Summing it all up, friends, I'd say you'll do best by filling your minds and meditating on things true, noble, reputable, authentic, compelling, gracious—the best, not the worst; the beautiful, not the ugly; things to praise, not things to curse." He then continued, "Do that, and God, who makes everything work together, will work you into His most excellent harmonies" (Philippians 4:8,9 MSG).

HAVE ANOTHER THOUGHT

You and I were wired "cable ready" for heaven. We were made to think the thoughts of the Lord, whose thoughts and words are so powerful. The Amplified version of Hebrews 4:12 says: "The word that God speaks is alive and full of power [making it active, operative, energizing and effective.]" Then the punch line: "penetrating the deepest parts of our nature." The things He reveals to us can transform even our deepest, darkest areas!

Various forms of meditation encourage people to empty their minds of all thoughts, awaiting a spontaneous flow of new thoughts. God's call for us to meditate is the exact opposite. Instead of *emptying* our minds, we *fill* them with His words and His thoughts. The biblical word for *meditate* has nothing to do with a blank mind. It actually means to mutter or talk to yourself.

Paul had this in mind when he said, "Think on these things" (Philippians 4:8). To "think on" means to "take inventory." Take a good long look at all that's yours. Your Father did not spare His own Son in restoring you. In addition to the amazing gift of Jesus, He has freely given you *all* things! *Every* spiritual blessing in the heavenly realms (Ephesians 1:3). Worry sees lack, overlooking what God has made obvious. It chooses to be oblivious, ignoring the provision, because it fails to see our faithful Father.

I love to receive new revelations from Father and see Him in fresh ways. Yet I also have an increasing desire to walk in the things He has already shown me. More than simply having an informed mind, I want a radically transformed heart. I don't simply want the title deed to the Promised Land; I want to live there! The "anxious-for-nothing-worry-free-zone" is more than a concept. It actually exists in the shadow of the Fearless One.

Worry has trust issues. It attempts to compensate for past mistakes by taking control. Dreading the thought that history will repeat itself, worriers resort to manipulation or intimidation in their attempt to "fail-proof" their future. Compliant friends and family members become chess pieces in the worrier's fearful schemes. This eventually takes its toll on relationships, as no one likes to feel used. Yet, the greatest expense is levied on the worrier.

Worry wears you out. It breeds performance and perfectionism. "I'm going to do better next time." "I won't let that happen again."

LIVING IN THE PLACE OF THE FATHER'S EMBRACE

Our Father's solution to fear is *not* perfectionism. It's His perfect love. His "perfect love casts out fear." Perfectionism amplifies fear. It lives in a self-critical torture chamber. And when we live in this world of torment, those close to us begin to feel they will never be "good enough" either. But His perfect love accepts us as we *receive* Him. We enter the world of *knowing we are accepted* in the Beloved.

Jesus said He was going to the Cross to prepare a place for us. He said it would be the same place from which He lives—in His Father's house. Not only was He making a way for us to go to heaven *later*, He was

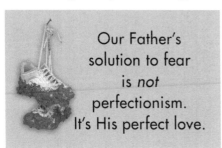

Our Father's solution to fear is *not* perfectionism. It's His perfect love.

making a way for us to live with His Father *now*. In the time He gave this promise, there was a custom many fathers observed. When their children married, the fathers would add more rooms to their homes. The newly married couples experienced a new place in the family. Jesus said, "In My Father's house there are *many* rooms." There is a place for you! I am making *My* place with My Father—*your* place, too. "Where I am—you may also be!"

John describes Jesus' "place" as living "in the bosom of the Father" (John 1:18 KJV). The term "bosom" is a picture of being in front of, face to face with, between the shoulders of and held in an embrace. Picture Jesus in the warm embrace of His Father. Can you see the smile on His face as He holds His beloved son, a son He is so pleased with? Now picture yourself in that same embrace. Jesus didn't simply say, "No one comes to Heaven but through Me." He said, "No one comes *to the Father* but through Me." He came to restore you to Father. The "place" He made for you is the place of the Father's embrace. In that place, perfect love drives every fear, every care and every worry far from us.

Life gets blurry in worry.

Things become clear when He is near.

ENDNOTE

1. Graham Cooke, *Radical Perceptions*, (Vancouver, WA: Brilliant Book House, 2011), 6.

CHAPTER NINE

Contentment

"God is most glorified in us when
we are most satisfied in Him."
– John Piper

I am forever in the process of learning new customs. My desire to connect with people in *their* world has given me a heightened awareness of what to do—and what *not* to do. Unfortunately most of my lessons are learned the hard way. A few years ago I was in Port-au-Prince, Haiti preparing to speak to a group of pastors. While seated on the platform in the front of a packed Haitian church building, I nervously crossed my legs as I placed my notes across my lap. The pastor in charge of the meeting tapped me on the shoulder and asked me to "uncross" my legs. He said if I showed the bottom of my shoe it was a sign of disrespect. Feeling embarrassed, I quickly placed both feet on the ground.

Soon the worship music began playing and all of us stood up to sing. After noticing that everyone else in the room was lifting their hands, I sheepishly raised mine, relieved to see this gesture was culturally acceptable. Yet once again the kindly host pastor tapped my shoulder. This time he advised, "It is not good to raise your hands while standing on this platform." "Why?" I asked, mortified I had once again violated protocol. With a wide grin he pointed to the apparatus whirring above my head. "Low ceiling fans," he replied, followed by a traditional Haitian chuckle.

CONTENTMENT AS A LIFESTYLE

Even more important than avoiding a cross-cultural faux pas is the eternal priority of learning the ways of the Kingdom. Paul encourages us to learn one of heaven's most vital priorities. He simply said, "I have learned to be content" (Philippians 4:11). In other words, "I've become accustomed to a new environment—one of total internal satisfaction." Discontent is the ultimate cultural faux pas in the Kingdom of God. It breaks the heart of our Father who "daily loads us with benefits" (Psalm 68:19 KJV).

Contentment is not being passive. It's not embodied by the 1950s Doris Day song, "Que Sera, Sera

(Whatever will be, will be)." It's not a shrug of the shoulders, a roll of the eyes, and an indifferent sigh that says, "Oh, *whatever!*"

We have been called to live far beyond "*Oh, whatever!*" We're called to a higher place. Rather than half-heartedly resigning ourselves to our circumstances, let's resist the trap of dissatisfaction and constant complaining by relying on the power of His strength within us.

Paul said, "Despite the circumstances, I have learned the secret. I have been instructed." Instruction is more than gaining information. It means to "put structure in." It's having a supernatural structure established inside of you. This edifice of super-abounding contentment causes us to stand firm. No matter what is going on around us, it cannot change the climate inside us. No one is *born* a pessimist. It is a learned trait. That's great news, because

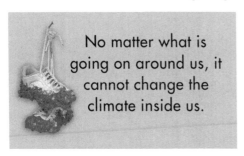

No matter what is going on around us, it cannot change the climate inside us.

it means this perspective can also be "*un*learned." It can be repented of and replaced. We can learn to turn our mind from earthly circumstances to heavenly perspectives.

DEPENDENCE AND INTERDEPENDENCE

From this place of contentment, Paul made two powerful statements. First, he made this declaration of dependence, "I can do all things through Christ who strengthens me" (Philippians 4:13 KJV 2000). Then he followed with another affirmation. He told his faithful friends, "I thank you that you were partakers with me in my trouble" (Philippians 4:14). This was a declaration of *inter*dependence.

We need God. *And* we need one another. We were never made to face life alone. These are not the days of the "Lone Rangers." These are times calling for the "Magnificent Seven" to ride together. It's the hour for God's people to *move as one*, in concert with the Holy Spirit.

One of God's earliest statements about us as human beings made in His image was, "It's not good for you to be alone." God knew this from experience. Our God is not just "He," our God is "we." In creation God said, "Let *us* make man in *our* image." Jesus, just before He died for us, prayed this for us: "That they may be one as *we* are one" (John 17:11). He longs for us to be united with Him and united with one another. Speaking of His relationship with Father and Holy Spirit, Jesus said, "*We* are one." We have come to call this the Trinity. Though the actual word does not appear in the Bible, it accurately describes "three who live in unity." Trinity is not simply a doctrine to be upheld, it's a *relationship* to be experienced. More than a divine organizational chart—it is a sign of mature love. Relationship at its highest level of loyalty and unity is displayed when

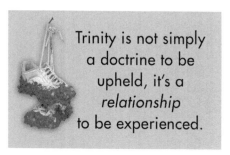

Trinity is not simply a doctrine to be upheld, it's a *relationship* to be experienced.

three distinct Persons flow as one, mutually depending on one another. We too can live in impenetrable contentment, with the help of our God and one another.

RESTING IN HIS PROMISES

We have been invited into the most deeply satisfying place. Jesus' invitation is this, "Come and abide in My words. Make your home in My promises. Let the revelation of My heart come alive inside of you. As you dwell in Me and dwell on My words, you will come to feel right at home in Me" (my paraphrase of John 15:7). Yet, Jesus warned us, "As you receive My words, the enemy's opposition may follow." His counsel, recorded in Matthew 13:21, warns us that "trouble and persecution" can come our way *because of* the word." The enemy is scared to death of us receiving the words of the Lord. Satan is especially terrified when we *believe* them. As we see who Jesus is, and who we really are because of Him, the enemy knows he is defeated. He is a liar. Lies are his only weapons, designed to keep us from knowing the truth. When opposition comes, we have a choice: we can receive the enemy's lies and accusing words (causing us to doubt the promises of God), or we can hold onto the revelation of God, finding our resting place in Him and riding out the storm.

Contented people absolutely crush the enemy's schemes. Divine contentment brings us into the place of peace—the place of undivided connection with the heart of our Father. In that place, the "God of peace" will literally "crush and completely shatter" the devil "under our feet" (Romans 16:20). Lucifer was utterly cast down from the heavenly place. He lost all connection with the Giver of Life and has been dying

Contented people absolutely crush the enemy's schemes.

a slow death ever since. Defeated and depleted, he works to spread his misery with whoever will receive it. But everyone who receives the Son receives His very life (1 John 5:12). While satan increasingly stagnates, we are supernaturally revitalized. In Jesus, we are inwardly being "renewed day by day" (2 Corinthians 4:16), and we are "continually made new in the attitude of [our] minds" (Ephesians 4:23). We are constantly being "transformed by the renewing of [our] mind[s]" (Romans 12:2). In this place of divine contentment, our joy depresses the enemy. Our rest rattles his cage. And our clear perspectives confuse him to the core. Our lack of frustration absolutely frustrates the devil's schemes.

RECKONING OURSELVES

In contentment, we can accurately assess who we are and all we have in Christ. We learn how to "reckon ourselves to be dead to sin but alive to God" (Romans 6:11). No, this is not a verse from the Cowboy Version of the Bible. The word "reckon" means

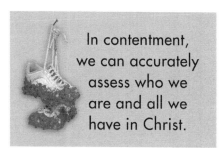

In contentment, we can accurately assess who we are and all we have in Christ.

to "take an inventory" and "make a conclusion." It's like recording the deposits that have been made in your banking accounts, making sure they are current. Imagine if you only had a few dollars to your name. You would live your life governed by a sense of lack. But what if someone deposited millions of dollars in your savings account? Until you update your files, you'll continue to live under the cloud of poverty. Only after you "reckon yourself," will you receive the upgraded assessment to lift you into new realms of abundance.

This natural illustration doesn't even come close to describing what the Father pours into the lives of His children. He promises all of His strength, ceaseless waves of His love and all of His presence. *His* quality of peace and joy and wisdom. At all times, He gives us all we need.

We become what we behold.

"As a man thinks in his heart, so is he" (Proverbs 23:7). We become what we behold. And increasing adoration of our amazing Father results in decreasing intimidation by the enemy. Satan simply cannot contend with contented ones.

CHAPTER TEN

Persevering

> *"Never give in.*
> *Never give in.*
> *Never, never, never, never—*
> *in nothing great or small,*
> *large or petty—*
> *never give in.*
> *Never yield to the*
> *apparently overwhelming*
> *might of the enemy."*
> – Winston Churchill

> *"Many of life's failures*
> *are people who did not realize*
> *how close they were to success*
> *when they gave up."*
> – Thomas Edison

> *"By perseverance*
> *the snail reached the ark."*
> – Charles H. Spurgeon

You were born to thrive in His Kingdom. You were not set up to let the world happen to you. You were sent to *happen to the world*. You have not been reduced to play the powerless victim role. Not for one minute! No, you have been raised to live powerfully—to "reign in this life" (Romans 5:17). And our Father supplies you with all you need to enjoy this abundantly confident life. He "daily loads you with benefits" (Psalm 16:18 NKJV). So much so, that "at all times" you will have "all you need" (2 Corinthians 9:8).

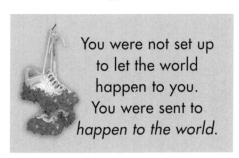

You were not set up to let the world happen to you. You were sent to *happen to the world*.

This doesn't mean our lives will be free from difficulties. Each of us will face unexpected setbacks in our preplanned schedules. Delays can be some of the most trying experiences we face. Between the moment God gives us a promise and the moment He brings fulfillment, the test of time can really test us. We can be tempted to "give out" in despair, to "give in" to disappointment, or to simply "give up" our hopes and dreams. Or we can position ourselves to receive the most amazing gifts our Father has for us in such seasons.

As we wait expectantly for Him, He gives us "new strength"—an increased capacity to trust Him and not be afraid. Rather than becoming victims of our circumstances, we can take responsibility for our lives. We've been made "response-able," given the ability to respond. So many of the Psalms reflect this response to His faithfulness. Though each song is unique, many of them follow this basic format:

–PART ONE–

INTIMACY. (Bishop Joseph Garlington calls this "into-me-see.") When we tell God what we are going through, and how we feel about it, He loves to meet with us "in the light." What touches us touches Him. In the Psalms this honest interaction is expressed in a variety of creative ways, i.e., "My bones are melting like wax. My soul is disturbed within me. Tears have been my food day and night. All my friends have left me. It even seems like God has forsaken me." If you thought Country Music cornered the market on sad songs, take a closer look!

–PART TWO–

REVELATION. In response to our honest expression of our hearts, the Lord brings an open expression of His heart. He enjoys filling us with memories of His faithfulness—from our personal experiences (i.e., He heard me, helped me, sheltered me) to the experiences of others (i.e., He parted the Red Sea).

–PART THREE–

PRAISE. His revelation inspires adoration. Out of a heart of renewed trust, our words express unhindered praise. The word frequently used for "praise" is *yada. Yada* is a verbal declaration that includes a physical demonstration. As I shared in a previous chapter, it means, "to thrust the uplifted hand." It often involves

His revelation inspires adoration.

a vigorous motion, like the propelling of a javelin. It was a way of stating to the Lord, "I thrust my life into Your presence. I cast my cares upon you." This "trust thrust" said, "I entrust all of my life to Your constant care!" At this point exuberant celebration would break out. Musicians would *selah*—a spontaneous instrumental expression of uninhibited adoration. Singers sang. Dancers danced. A party of praise erupted as the joy of the Lord became their strength.

–PART FOUR–

GOD'S RESPONSE. His answers from heaven are "above and beyond all we could ask or think" (Ephesians 3:20). Psalm 42 begins with the cry, "My soul is thirsty for God." God's response? "Deep calls to deep." The depths of His children's cry rouse the deepest places in His heart. He responds to their desire for refreshing with much more than a mere trickle of living water. He gives them wild waterfalls. He comes with mighty waves of His presence. On top of that He brings "breakers"—literally "water-spouts and tornadoes!" They asked Him for water. And He gave them a waterpark!

The songwriter cries, "All Your waves and break-ers have swept over me" (Psalm 42:7). The phrase

Connecting with Him at the heart level changes everything.

"swept over" is the picture of a boat completely filled with water and going under. In the natural, this looks like a tragedy, but in the spirit it is amaz-ing. It's an image of being completely engulfed in His atmosphere. Sinking in His presence. Once ensnared by our circumstance, we suddenly find ourselves overwhelmed by our Father's love.

"By day He directs His love." His love is relent-less. It's directed to the places of our greatest need as He heals our broken hearts. He persistently pours out revelations of His compassion toward us. "At night His song is with us." We suddenly find our waking and resting moments completely consumed with His presence. What is "His song?" It is "a prayer to the

God of my life"—an unbroken connection to and conversation with the One our soul loves to be with.

HEART TO HEART

Connecting with Him at the heart level changes everything. Two of Jesus' friends experienced this. Unknowingly walking beside Him after He had risen from the dead, they later commented, "Didn't our hearts burn within us as He talked with us on the way?" (Luke 12:42).  When His hearts touches ours we are never the same. We can't stay "stuck" in the same place. Peter called it being *"moved by* the Holy Spirit" (2 Peter 1:21). Where is He taking us? He moves us *beyond passivity* into the *realm of perseverance.* We are brought into a place where we will not quit. We will not back off. We will not back down. No matter what *has happened* or what *is happening*—we refuse to be quitters!

Perseverance is the power to overcome weariness—the strength to "not give up" (Luke 18:1). Weariness is much more than being physically tired. Being "weary" means you just don't want to try again. Weary people have given up and given in to mental and emotional

Perseverance is the power to overcome weariness.

indifference. But that is *not* who we are. We have been made to be overcomers. Jesus' call to everyone with a "weary" soul is, "Come to Me." I will heal your soul. Here in My presence you will discover "rest for your souls"—the deep-settled confidence in knowing I am worth trusting (Matthew 11:28).

James said the words of God to us are like a "mirror" (James 1:22-25). They give us a clear reflection of who we really are in Him. With this in mind, consider this declaration of your true identity from Hebrews 10:39, "We are not of those who shrink back and are destroyed, but of those who believe and are saved." To "shrink back" speaks of a slow, steady, subtle retreat. It feigns faith, but deep within it has already forfeited the battle. But that is *not* who we are! "We are those who believe. We are deeply convicted. Fully persuaded. Saved and restored through and through. As a result, we are abundantly possessing all that is ours" (my paraphrase of Hebrews 10:39b).

PERSEVERING

Hebrews 6:12 says, "You won't become lazy but will be imitators of those who inherit the promises *through faith and perseverance*" (HCSB). We need faith. And we need perseverance. We need faith to *believe* the promises God has made, and we need perseverance to trust *until* we *receive* the promises God has made. Perseverance is our posture between the "now" and the "not yet." It's the capacity to hold fast to what He has said "now," though the manifestation has "not yet" happened.

Paul describes the attitude of perseverance as "straining toward what is ahead" (Philippians 3:13). Picture athletes running toward the finish line of a foot race, every muscle taut. With a look of sheer determination on each face, they sprint toward the ribbon. Every last drop of energy is being expended. Nothing is being held back. That's straining!

It's the look I've seen on the face of Sheri, my wife, as she worked hard to bring our three children into the world. (The word "labor" has a whole new meaning to me now.) We attended the prenatal classes and learned how to breathe "Lamaze" style. This puffing

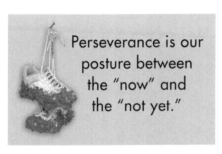

Perseverance is our posture between the "now" and the "not yet."

and panting pattern of metered breathing only left me lightheaded. I wondered if it actually accomplished something. Or did the medical team invent it as a way to make young fathers hyperventilate and pass out, so they could remove them from the delivery room?

We were taught the importance of a focal point. Delivering mothers need to keep their eyes and mind centered on one thing. We chose my face. I'm not sure if that was a wise idea. Sheri wanted my face to be smiling. All the time. Our first delivery took over 18 hours. I have never smiled so long in all my life. (And I thought smiling for wedding pictures was grueling!)

Perseverance has a focal point: our eyes are fixed on Jesus. Our hearts stay focused on the One who has given us promises, knowing He is faithful and He will bring it to pass. The writer of Hebrews said, "Throw off everything that hinders. Let's run the race with perseverance" (Hebrews 12:1). The "race" referred to here is a marathon. A contest. A battle. "Fight the good fight of faith" (1 Timothy 6:12) could be translated more clearly as "wage a good warfare of faith." It's more than "one punch and you're done, one shout and it's over, or one Scripture and it's through." There is persistence. Perseverance. A determination that says, "We are going to get there. We will see the goodness of the Lord in the land of the living!" Many are stuck in disappointment simply because they did not plan for the long haul.

Weariness lowers the standard of expectancy. Weary people often adopt a theology based on their disappointment with God. Weary ones say with a shrug, "Oh well, I guess that's all I can expect in this life. I'll simply endure the earth and experience heaven later." But perseverance says, "By the grace of God, I am going to see as much of heaven invade this life as I possibly can." There are gaps in this life between the "now" and the "not yet." Promises have been made, yet they have not fully manifested. Weary people accept and accommodate the gaps. But persevering people stand in the gap and say, "Come, Kingdom of God. Be done, will of God." They replace the "Oh, well" of weariness with the "Thy will be done" of expectancy.

DIRECTING OUR HEARTS INTO HIS LOVE

There are many things I have been longing to see for years. There are dimensions of His will that aren't fully realized in my life. When I hear "give thanks in every circumstance; for *this is God's will for you* in Christ Jesus" (1 Thessalonians 5:18), I say, "Let *Your will* be done in my life." There is still a gap in me. I love to give Him thanks. I need His help in the "in every circumstance" department.

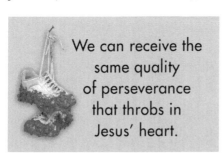

We can receive the same quality of perseverance that throbs in Jesus' heart.

When I catch myself (or I'm caught) complaining, He calls me to resist the "Oh, well" (i.e., "Everybody complains. You'll never beat it. Just accept it as normal behavior.") and declare, "Thy will. Make me a grateful son. Fill my heart with thanksgiving." We can be so renewed in the atmosphere of our thought life that we can prove (unmistakably demonstrate) what His "good, pleasing and perfect will" is (Romans 12:2).

Perseverance could easily become a tedious exercise in self-righteous performance. Yet sheer determination on our part can never produce perseverance in our heart. Only our Father can do that. He opens this amazing door of opportunity to us, "May the Lord direct your hearts into God's love and Christ's perseverance" (2 Thessalonians 3:5). The New Living Translation of this same promise says:

> *"May the Lord lead your hearts into a full understanding and expression of the love of God and the patient endurance that comes from Christ."*

We can experience the Father's embrace, as His loves releases us from all fear. And we can receive the same quality of perseverance that throbs in Jesus' heart, empowering us to experience a hope that endures.

He completes what He starts in you.

He never quits.

He loves to fill you with His tenacity.

CHAPTER ELEVEN

Beyond Defeat

> *"It's not the load that breaks you down,*
> *it's the way you carry it."*
> – Lena Horne

> *"But I thank God, who always*
> *leads us in victory because of Christ."*
> – 2 Corinthians 2:14

"Though a righteous man falls (or *fails, is overwhelmed*) seven times, he rises again" (Proverbs 24:16a). This promise became a lifeline to me in a season of personal defeat.

Each component of this proverb is worth noting. Being righteous refers to enjoying a thriving relationship with God. The number seven frequently symbolizes "totality" or "being complete." So falling "seven times" is a picture representing thorough disappointment—a complete setback.

My paraphrase of this wise saying goes something like this: *When you feel like you have been a total failure—when it seems all hope is gone—out of your relationship with God you can get back on your feet again. And instead of being a "set-up" for the next devastation, you will experience the capacity to go higher. You will rise to a place superior to the one you fell from. A moment appearing to be utter disaster can give way to a season of total restoration. And that restoration speaks of receiving more than what was lost.* This is more than a cliché or dry concept. It has become reality to me—one the Holy Spirit has reminded me of again and again.

CORRIE AND ME

I was twelve years old when I first heard Corrie ten Boom speak. This gentle woman with a Dutch accent and a warm smile won my heart. She and her family owned a clock shop in Holland during the early days of the Holocaust,

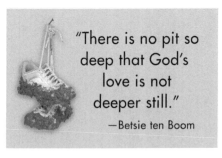

"There is no pit so deep that God's love is not deeper still."

—Betsie ten Boom

and they harbored Jewish refugees in a "hiding place" within the walls of their home. Eventually their efforts were discovered by the Nazi regime and

Corrie, her sister and father were arrested. Though both of her family members died during the incarceration, by amazing grace Corrie survived the horrors of Ravensbruck death camp, one of the harshest Nazi concentration facilities. Just before her sister, Betsie, died there, she spoke these powerful words to Corrie, "There is no pit so deep that God's love is not deeper still."

Corrie carried these words. Though she faced deep pits of physical and mental torture, she discovered the "still deeper" realms of God's supply. He sustained her in the horrors of a Nazi death camp, and orchestrated her release just days before her scheduled execution in the gas chambers. Throughout the rest of her life, Corrie traveled the world encouraging people to trust God in the face of overwhelming difficulty.

On that evening many years ago, in a little white church building near my hometown, Corrie spoke to my heart. I was so impacted by her words that I eventually purchased my one and only "pin-up" poster that ever hung in my bedroom. It was a picture of Corrie ten Boom accompanied by her sister's famous quote: "There is no pit so deep that God's love is not deeper still." Little did I know the many opportunities I would have to discover the incredible depth of His love.

THE EARLY YEARS

Sheri and I were two college friends who fell in love. We married in the summer of 1978, and next to following Jesus, it was the best choice I have ever made. Her warmth and wit, her dreams and passion for life, her practical no-nonsense ways—all combined to deeply attract my heart. We started out as newlyweds on a shoestring budget, but with hearts chock-full of hope. While fixing up a 100-year-old home, we also invested in the journey of becoming one. Sheri worked in a local Christian bookstore while I attended a nearby seminary and delivered kitchen cabinets on weekends.

A few months into married life, we received an offer from the United Methodist church. The pastor of two small churches was seriously ill and in need of a replacement. After a few days of prayer and discussion, we agreed to walk with them. Proud stewards of a pair of country churches, we stepped into the wild and woolly world of shepherding His sheep. And wild it was. Calling it a "learning experience" would be an understatement!

At twenty-two years old I was a new husband and an inexperienced pastor. My heart was filled with visions of a vibrant, healthy Church bringing Jesus' healing love to the world. Though not yet visible, I knew we could see this materialize. In my youthful zeal I thought I could change a church in a week, maybe even in five days! But reality brought me a rude awakening as my enthusiastic dreams clashed with established traditions. Since that time I've learned that I made many mistakes common to young leaders. I spent most of my energy attempting to be *understood,* yet very little in seeking to *understand* the hearts and history of the people. I thought I knew more than most of the members, even the seasoned ones. I was so wrong. "Change" became my middle name as I sought to shift the culture overnight. From worship expressions to bold adventures with the Holy Spirit, I wanted these churches to experience it all, yet failed to realize that my pace was wearying them.

It was quite some time before anyone provided feedback on my efforts, either positive or negative. Still I forged ahead, oblivious to the gap forming between us. Then times of spiritual awakening began, during which a local drug dealer surrendered his heart to Jesus. Soon others followed. Before long the "new people" in the church outnumbered the founding core. The older members were terrified by this growing company of "radicals," and felt as if they were losing their church. Yet I was so elated with signs of new life, I overlooked the mounting walls of division. From the perspective of the seasoned church members and leaders, I didn't seem to care.

Before long I was faced with a dilemma: should I slow my pace, alter my convictions or resign? Realizing that most of the official membership was not in agreement with my vision, I made the painful decision to resign. Rather than "split" a church, I thought I would slip away into the night, lick my wounds and await the next opportunity.

THE AFTERMATH

The season that followed was bittersweet, to say the least. Bitter were the regrets. In retrospect there were a number of lessons learned concerning things I wish I had done differently. But leaders don't have the luxury of making mistakes in seclusion. The most difficult issue for me to face was how my immaturity had hurt others—an issue I would need God's grace to resolve.

Sweet was the discovery that many people had been helped by our years together. They had been healed, rescued and restored to their heavenly Papa. I am continually amazed at how He moves through us, in spite of our humanness. Feeling a strong connection to this company of people, we sensed a responsibility to care for them. Their inability to return to the former church coupled with their constant requests for us to return to pastor them tugged at my heart. Before long, whether wise or unwise, we agreed to start a new church with whoever desired to join us. We rented a ballroom in a hotel, purchased some cribs and a sound system, and began meeting on Sundays.

Yet, my heart was still wounded from the recent flurry of events. In a decision made out of rebound instincts, I appealed to an outside ministry to consider "covering" us. I still felt shaken by the years of feeling that I carried sole responsibility for our former church situation. Nagging insecurity clouded my discernment. Failure to count the cost before journeying with another ministry compounded our already troubled situation. As we proceeded, our divergent core values became increasingly evident. Eventually a painful decision on the part of our newfound overseers led them to remove me from all pastoral responsibilities. Numb and disillusioned from all that had transpired, I walked away from leading this newly formed church. Though we continued to attend as members, we had no involvement in its leadership. Weeks turned to months, which grew to more than two years of meetings, during which I was continually reminded of a life gone by.

I found a job at a nursing home where I served as a social worker and later as the admissions director. In many ways I was glad to be away from the daily grind of church life. I've heard it said, "Sheep can bite." I've also heard, "Shepherds can barbeque." I experienced both. Serving among the residents at the retirement center, I was in some sense "safe": at least most of them didn't bite. Their false teeth often rested safely in a glass beside their beds.

Perhaps the most crushing blow to my spirit came from the mouths of leaders. As I was leaving my position as pastor, they told me I had no business being a leader in the church. They questioned both my sense of calling as well as my ability to serve. One overseer put it bluntly, "You are not a pastor. Never should have been. Never will be." With those words I allowed my dreams to die. I shut down, emotionally. I locked the study in the basement of our house, and with it I locked up my heart, vowing I'd never risk getting hurt in the church arena again.

THE HEALING

I began the process of training to become a nursing home administrator, filled with a desire to honor the aging, an audience often neglected. We left the church we had pastored and began attending a Dove Fellowship church, a congregation founded by our friends, Larry and Laverne Kreider. This warm company of believers led by their wonderful pastor Ron Myer brought us into a place of healing. Though I initially held myself back at arm's length, the sincere love of this church family chipped away at my hardened heart.

One particular Sunday morning I had an encounter with Father's love that would forever transform the way I face personal defeat. As the worship rose from hearts around the room, the ice surrounding my soul began to melt. I had so guarded myself from further disappointment that I rarely laughed or shed a tear. Deep inside, my love had grown cold. Yet on this day, every song that was sung and every spoken word seemed directed at me. I fought back the tears, attempting to suppress my volatile emotions.

Following the worship gathering, Sheri mingled with lots of people. Being nine months pregnant  with Brandon, our third child, there were many who wanted to talk with her and pray for her. I stood like a statue along the back wall. Hearing their jovial dialogue only served to further irritate my inner turmoil. Arms crossed against my chest, I assumed the "don't talk to me" stance.

Troubles don't last forever. Defeats are not final.

But a young man in his mid-teens began to talk to me, anyway. He had Downs Syndrome and one of the warmest smiles I've ever seen. "Hi," he said, grinning ear to ear. "God talk to me about you," he continued. "Pastor Ron said God talk to us. And sometimes He tell us things about other people. He told me something about you." Again, he smiled, projecting a sincerity that was thawing my frosty heart.

"What did He tell you?" I asked, feeling disarmed and intrigued. "He told me you a pastor. You a pastor!" With a shadow of sadness moving across his face he continued, "Some men told you you not a pastor." But quickly the smile returned, "But you *are* pastor. God call you pastor. We need you to be pastor again."

Then this young man embraced me, wrapping his arms around me as if he never meant to let go. If you've ever spent time with Downs children, you'll vividly recall their capacity for affection. Throughout his unflinching demonstration of love he would throw his head back, look straight into my eyes, smile with abandon and then go right back to hugging. His affection was too much for me to withstand, and my dormant tear ducts gave way to uncontrollable gushes of water. I returned his embrace, burying my face in the top of his head.

This exchange was more than a young man's obedience to the voice of God. It was my heavenly Father drawing me to Himself. This was my Papa telling me, "You're My son. I delight in you. No matter what you've done or how you've failed. Regardless of all your regrets, you are Mine. You are not disqualified, because I have called you. I have qualified you. And My gifts and My calling have not been taken from you. My call on your life is irrevocable."

Chains that bound me to bitter memories of defeat were removed from my heart that day. Certainly my performance since then has not been flawless. As a husband, father, brother, son, friend and leader, I have disappointed people in every role I fill. And yet I've discovered the joy of not allowing my performance to define me or confine me. Though it has been many years since the young man hugged me at the church in Newmanstown, Pennsylvania, I have lived with an ever-increasing sense of our Father's embrace. His love released me from regretful clutches of defeat. At this writing, I have spent over two decades pastoring a wonderful family of believers. While the earlier season of defeat seems like a faint memory, at the time it seemed to be an ominous prison from which I'd never escape. In light of His prevailing purposes, it joins the ranks of things that may have come, but just as surely "came to pass." Troubles don't last forever. Defeats are not final.

He will always lead us into His ultimate triumph!

If you are presently stuck in the place of defeat and personal disappointment, take heart. This will not be your endless condition. Though you may not have a person waiting to physically embrace you, you do have a Father who is ready to fully restore you. He loves to speak truth to your deepest places, releasing you from lies that bind and establishing you in His realities of freedom. He will set you back on your feet and return you to the right pathways. He will always lead us into His ultimate triumph!

CHAPTER TWELVE

Beyond Wounds

"By His wounds we are healed."
– Isaiah 53:5

*"All praise to the God and Father
of our Master, Jesus the Messiah!
Father of all mercy!
God of all healing counsel!
He comes alongside us when
we go through hard times,
and before you know it,
he brings us alongside someone
else who is going through
hard times so that we can
be there for that person
just as God was there for us.
We have plenty of hard times
that come from following the Messiah,
but no more so than the good times
of his healing comfort—
we get a full measure of that, too."*
– 2 Corinthians 1:3-4, The Message

The first time I saw her, she was sitting on the floor, nearly hidden in the back corner of a room overflowing with people. I was ministering in Hyderabad, India, and among the ocean of faces, hers arrested my attention. Fragments of a story were being divulged by her eyes—one filled with pain, rage and shame. Something deeply wounding had happened. Something of which she was ashamed. Something her face could no longer conceal.

We were gathered in the ministry complex of our friends Mohan and Rani Babu. The Babus' zeal for Jesus is obvious and contagious. As well as surrendering their lives in love for others, every inch of their physical property is also utilized. Their land encompasses an orphanage, a Bible school to prepare men and women for ministry, and a large church building. Needless to say, it's always abuzz with activity. In the warm Indian climate, laughter often punctuates the air, rising above the hum of the continual interaction of friends.

That afternoon was sweltering. If you thought a slight breeze was stirring, it was merely your imagination. The air in our crowded meeting was still, but God was active! Hope was rising and faith was increasing, empowering people to trust and receive His promises and their fulfillment. By the end of the meeting, I was exhausted. We had just arrived hours earlier, after twenty-four hours of travel. Then suddenly standing in front of me was the girl from the corner of the room. I motioned for her to move closer. Alongside me were the pastor and an interpreter, with whom I'd formed an immediate bond as we prayed for people that afternoon. Our hearts broke as she staggered forward with awkward and painful motions, which made the infirmity pervading her body obvious. Her eyes filled with a mixture of pain and sadness, and they seemed to plead, "Help me."

Compassion surged through me like a pent-up flood. I've always loved the accounts of Jesus being "moved by compassion" as He healed those who were sick. This day I experienced His empathetic love beating through my heart. His gift of faith came upon us, too, as He lifted us into His unlimited capacity to bring restoration. I knew faith was rising in this young girl's heart, because I could see it reflected in her eyes. The glazed look of disappointment with life was being edged out by flashes of expectancy and hope. The same eyes, once crying for help, were now shouting, "I *know* God can help me!"

We listened as unreserved words began flowing from her mouth in rhythms unique to the Telugu language. Communicating through translation has some wonderful benefits. It slows the pace of interaction and makes room for increased observation. Even before I heard the translator's interpretation of this young girl's story, her agony became real to me. Her eyes flared as her voice swelled, every word seeming to punctuate her torment.

The translator turned to us, and in her articulately metered words began to unfold the story. An alcoholic single mother brought this girl into the world. Unwanted since birth, her mother would frequently vent life's frustrations on this innocent child. Caught up in a drunken rage, one night she used a wooden club to silence her two-year-old daughter's crying. The repeated blows inflicted multiple fractures on both legs, permanently crippling this little girl. Because medical attention was never sought, the broken bones set improperly. As her daughter grew, the bones in her legs fused in a twisted sequence, making walking nearly impossible. Her waddling style of maneuvering caught the attention of other children in her neighborhood, and various names of ridicule became her designated identity. She was taunted daily. Unwanted, ridiculed and crippled, her outer wounds only mirrored the deep devastation to her soul.

But this day was different. Hope touched her heart as her heavenly Father drew her to Himself. Expectancy that a new life was possible streamed into her soul. This day would bring radical change.

We prayed a simple prayer, first declaring Jesus' ability and desire to heal her, followed by a command to her body to receive His healing love. In my earliest religious training I had been taught to pray with my eyes closed, born out of a desire to assist with focus and remove distractions. Yet on this day I kept my eyes open, and I'm so glad I did. As I watched in wonder, her disfigured legs straightened and her withered muscles inflated right before my eyes. Looking into her face was a miracle all its own. Utter joy displaced the shame once shrouding her.

Then she took her first step. Like a child learning to walk for the first time, she gingerly moved her feet across the floor. And then the realization dawned on her: she had new legs! Her waddling days were gone. Her pace accelerated and before long, she was almost jogging back and forth across the room. Others gathered to behold this amazing sight, forming two lines and clapping as she paced back and forth between them. She looked like the featured performer on a dance floor.

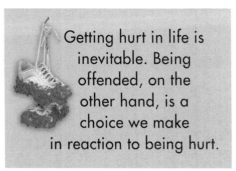

Getting hurt in life is inevitable. Being offended, on the other hand, is a choice we make in reaction to being hurt.

With exuberance she repeatedly shouted a phrase in Telugu. Because I was unfamiliar with her native tongue, I asked the translator what she was saying. I was certain she was declaring, "I can walk. I can walk!" But I was wrong. "She keeps saying, 'I forgive her! I forgive her!'" the translator grinned. I was stunned. Though obviously elated with her newfound ability to move unhindered, this girl's greater joy came from her transformed heart! She was now able to love her mother unobstructed by bitterness. More than physical freedom, she was most grateful to be released from the prison of unforgiveness.

Disappointment is often fueled by the inability to forgive others. Jesus described the life of an unforgiving person as someone living in a penitentiary, experiencing endless torment (Matthew 18:34,35). Getting hurt in life is inevitable. Being offended, on the other hand, is a choice we make in reaction to being hurt.

People can warm our hearts with their love, but they can also wound our hearts with their selfishness. At times the very same people can either hurt us or heal us. The same father who attended all your baseball games may never have

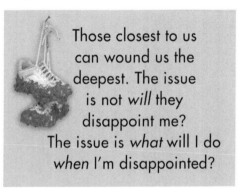

Those closest to us can wound us the deepest. The issue is not *will* they disappoint me? The issue is *what* will I do when I'm disappointed?

said, "I love you" or "I'm so proud of you." The same spouse who promises to "love and cherish" you "till death do us part" can also crush your heart with rejection or infidelity. Those closest to us can wound us the deepest. The issue is not *will* they disappoint me? The issue is *what* will I do *when* I'm disappointed? That afternoon in Hyderabad, a young woman received Jesus' healing grace, empowering her to live free from resentment. He really does "heal the brokenhearted, binding up their wounds" (Psalm 147:3).

Moving beyond our wounding is vital to both our personal growth as well as our connection to others. Until we face our pain and receive His healing, we will live superficial lives, and our ministry to others will be severely limited. The Lord addressed this issue when He challenged Israel to cease from treating "the wound of My people as if it were not serious. 'Peace, peace,' they say, when there is no peace" (Jeremiah 8:11). Wounds do not heal by simply ignoring them.

The issue of receiving healing for our offenses is crucial to God. In Leviticus 21:20, it's recorded that the Lord instructed Israel to prohibit anyone from serving as a priest if they had open, unhealed wounds. This same principle applies to us today as members of His royal priesthood. We cannot minister effectively to others with an unhealed soul. Our most important ministry tool is our heart. Out of the condition of our heart we impact the hearts of others. Solomon instructs, "Above all else, guard your heart, for everything you do flows from it" (Proverbs 4:23).

Since we minister to people out of the overflow of our lives, ignoring our unhealed wounds will greatly hinder ministry. Wounded people serve others from a performance vantage point—doing things *for acceptance* rather than serving selflessly *from a place of being accepted by God*. Those carrying emotional wounds are deeply insecure. To compensate, they feel a need to *have a ministry* rather than *simply minister* to the needs of others. An insatiable need to *prove their worth* trumps *improving other people's sense of their personal value*. The basic issue appears to be this: unhealed people *use people*, while healed people purely *love people*.

When we are healed, the place of our greatest wounding becomes the base for our greatest ministry. In that place, our Father imparts a deep deposit

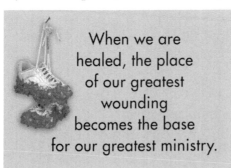

When we are healed, the place of our greatest wounding becomes the base for our greatest ministry.

of compassion and authority to bring healing to others. Jesus, fresh from His resurrection, still had wounds in His body. But they weren't open wounds. They were scars—healed wounds. His disciple Thomas was struggling to believe Jesus was alive again. Having watched Him die a gruesome death, Thomas' grief was immense and his shame was intense in light of his abandoning Jesus during His arrest. Jesus told Thomas to touch His scars, a gesture leaving no room for doubt about His love for him. People with open wounds don't let anyone get close to them, lest they get hurt again. But those whose wounds have healed seek to bring the same restoration to others.

Jesus' scars represented more than Roman punishment. He received the penalty we each deserved, not simply for our crimes against humanity, but even more for our defiant revolt against God's rightful reign over us. Isaiah 53:5 explains it this way, "But He was pierced for our transgressions. He was crushed for our iniquities. The punishment that brought us peace was upon Him, and by His stripes we are healed." Jesus' wounds were far more than physical. He *carried our sorrows*. He *carried the grief* we caused Him when we rejected Him. If one person's rejection of us can crush our hearts in disappointment—and if just one hurtful word deeply grieves the Holy Spirit— imagine what all of humanity's revolt against God felt like to Him! It's hard to comprehend what the words, "His wounds," fully mean. His open wounds could be a place of eternal shaming. He would have every right to continually humiliate us by scowling and saying, "Just look what you've done to Me." Instead

He smiles, showing us His healed wounds, and says, "Look what I've done *for* you."

For every wound you have ever received, there is an abundance of healing mercies available to you. He comforts us in our wounded places with much more than a warm feeling. Comfort literally means to "come fortify," as He strengthens us in places weakened through offense. Listen to this amazing promise:

> *"Father of mercies and God of all comfort, who comforts us in **all our afflictions** so that **we will be able to comfort** those who are in any affliction with the comfort with which we ourselves are comforted by God. For just as the sufferings of Christ are ours in abundance, so also **our comfort is abundant through Christ"*** (2 Corinthians 1:3-5, NAS).

There are deep deposits of comfort inside of you, received in your most painful moments. There are wounded people around you waiting to receive the same comfort you were given.

Several years ago I battled leukemia (the complete story is recorded in my first book, *Hope Beyond Reason*). For the better part of a year I was incapacitated, missing significant events in our children's lives. Today, I am healed. My body is cancer-free and my soul has been restored from the effects of fear and disappointment. My scars are now places of fresh sensitivity to others battling similar diseases. My healed wounds are now centers of greater authority to stand with them as Jesus brings healing. I frequently have opportunities to meet with others diagnosed with cancer, and we often experience an immediate connection. A thankful look says, "You understand! You've been where I am." Great doors of opportunity have opened for me to cry with, listen to, pray for and stand

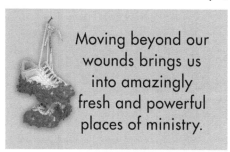

Moving beyond our wounds brings us into amazingly fresh and powerful places of ministry.

with suffering people. Moving beyond our wounds brings us into amazingly fresh and powerful places of ministry.

CHAPTER THIRTEEN

A New Place

*"God can deliver you so well that some
people won't believe your testimony."*
— Shannon L. Alder

*"When the Lord brought back the captive
ones of Zion, we were like those who dream."*
— Psalm 126:1

We can so accommodate our lives to being disheartened that it becomes normal, even comfortable, to anticipate disappointment. There is a counterfeit comfort in excusing ourselves from responsibility because we're overwhelmed with life. Yet we've been made to live powerful lives. In Him we are *"more than conquerors,"* and His power is more than able to bring us into victory over even the most traumatizing experiences.

John was called "the disciple whom Jesus loved." This epithet wasn't started because Jesus played favorites; it indicated that John had learned how to receive His love. John got it! In fact he so owned his place in Father's affection that *he referred to himself as the 'loved disciple' in his own Gospel* (John 20:2). He knew how to live loved, regardless of his circumstances. And that capacity to rest in Father's love would one day be tested to extreme measures.

Giving an account of his later years, John states with simplicity, "I was on the island of Patmos" (Revelation 1:9). Without a little historical context, you might miss the significance of those seven innocuous words. Patmos was a Roman prison camp—a slave penitentiary overseen by some of the cruelest people who ever walked the earth. Romans were known for their horrendous treatment of others, especially those viewed as a threat to their regime. John, seen as a Christian radical, clearly fell into the Roman category of an "enemy of the state." Yet despite his hostile environment, John experienced heaven in the midst of a hellish situation. He called that moment "the Lord's day." I believe that more than referencing a day of the week, he was referring to the state of the day. It was "the *Lord's* day!" Though the Romans assumed they were in charge of John, the island and the empire, John was declaring the supremacy of Jesus and His reign, as well as the Lord's governance over the day.

In describing the remarkable encounter he had on this day, John said, "*Immediately* I was in the Spirit."

He didn't leave Patmos. He wasn't voted off the island. In one moment he was present to all the pain of Patmos, and in the next he was *immediately* present to the presence of God. The word "immediately" means "at once into a new place." Instantaneously

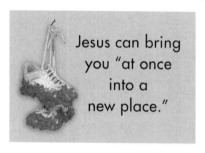

Jesus can bring you "at once into a new place."

he was moved to a new place with a new perspective. Suddenly the most amazing revelation filled his heart as He saw Jesus seated on His throne, ruling in absolute authority over all things. This revelation moved John to see life from heaven's perspective. The words he recorded of his encounter with Jesus that day are referred to as "The Revelation of Jesus Christ to John." It's not called "the revelation of the end times" or "the revelation of the antichrist." It is the revelation of Jesus Christ. Just as this revelation of Jesus put John's present situation into proper perspective, it also puts human history into heaven's perspective. The culmination of all antiquity will be the ultimate reign of Jesus and His kingdom!

Since Jesus is the same *today* as He was with John *that day*, He can bring the same revelation of His presence to you right now! He may not pluck you from the challenges of your immediate circumstance, but He can cause you to be "immediate" to Him. He can bring you "at once into a new place."

I love the Body of Christ—the fellowship of friends who follow Jesus. I love the mutual encouragement, the collective wisdom and the corporate support of His amazing family. We shouldn't reduce statements like, "It is not good for man to be alone" and "Two are better than one," to being thought of as endorsements by God for marriage. In a broader sense, they capture His commentary on the importance of community. In Paul's words, "We all belong to each other" (Romans 12:5 NLT). Arrogantly *independent* people deny this, their self-sufficiency keeping them relationally distant. Overly *dependent* people exploit relationships, resigning their responsibility to make decisions, and imposing it on others. Instead, we have been made for healthy *interdependence*, both receiving input *and* taking responsibility for our lives.

We have been made for healthy *interdependence,* both receiving input *and* taking responsibility for our lives.

Getting "unstuck" from disappointment is not simply a corporate responsibility. In order to fully experience this freedom, each of us must make the choices necessary to escape its grip. One of King David's most disheartening experiences was also his loneliest. Returning with his army to their hometown, David and his men were shocked to discover their abode devastated by an Amalekite attack. Their fierce enemies had destroyed their homes and captured their families. All of the men wept until they could wail no longer. Then, they turned their anger on David, blaming him for the tragedy. David, rejected and alone, did this one atmosphere-altering maneuver: he "strengthened himself in the Lord" (1 Samuel 30:6). No one could do this for him. In taking responsibility to receive the Lord's strength in his weak moment, David shifted the climate. As a result, the rest of his men were inspired by David's contagious courage. They arose, pursued and destroyed their enemies, then rescued their families. Not one of them was lost!

David's way of handling crises is a wise example for us to follow. We must *first* take responsibility for *our* actions, remembering that we have the "ability to respond" in situations like these. Can you recall your grade school teacher's instructions during a test? "Keep your eyes on your own paper. No talking during the test. Remember what you've been taught." There are tests no one else can take for us. Your test is your time to discover who you are in Him and who He is in you. Staying focused on your assignment and avoiding "the comparison trap" will help. Refrain from too many conversations with others (i.e., complaining sessions), and instead spend time "in the Lord" strengthening yourself in Him. Each test is an opportunity for the Holy Spirit both to teach you something new as well as remind you of what you've already been taught.

No one knows the specifics of what occurred in those moments David spent in the secret place with the Lord, but it certainly wasn't a one-sided conversation. Perhaps

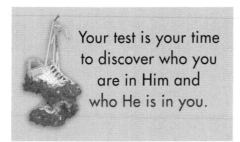

Your test is your time to discover who you are in Him and who He is in you.

David began by reminding himself of God's incredible faithfulness to him over the years. In those moments the Lord also reminded him of His deep love for His son. The warm touch of a loved one deeply ministers to us. Yet only our Father can so deeply embrace our soul that every fear is put to flight. There our soul finds rest—a deep abiding reassurance that we are fiercely and fervently loved by One who will never turn away. In His secret place we are reminded we are never alone, always guarded and forever loved. Only we can choose to enter that place and abide there. Others cannot do it for us, and God will never force Himself upon us. Freedom to choose is one of His greatest gifts to us.

No one can control you. Not your trials, the opinions of others, or even your own emotions. His grace empowers you to stop the spiral of panic, reflect on His faithfulness, and receive renewed strength. By His grace you can make clear choices that clear the way for His breakthrough. Like John the Baptist, you too can "prepare the way" for the Lord to intervene and bring you into a new place—one filled with His encouraging presence.

CHAPTER FOURTEEN

Living Beyond Disappointment

"Weeping may last through the night,
but joy comes with the morning."
– Psalm 30:5, NLT

"When a woman gives birth,
she has a hard time,
there's no getting around it.
But when the baby is born,
there is joy in the birth.
This new life in the world
wipes out memory of the pain.
The sadness you have right now
is similar to that pain,
but the coming joy is also similar.
When I see you again, you'll be full of joy,
and it will be a joy no one can rob from you.
You'll no longer be so full of questions."
– Jesus,
as quoted in John 16:21-23, The Message

Disappointment can feel like the end, but it doesn't have to be. It can actually be the beginning! You may say, "That seems *impossible*! How can anything good come out of what I'm going through?" God *loves* to reveal Himself in difficult situations. We view them as impossible, but He doesn't. *Nothing* is impossible in His eyes (Luke 1:37). He absolutely enjoys moving in unlikely ways through unlikely people in unlikely circumstances. His redemptive work is so remarkable

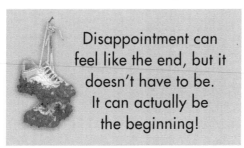

Disappointment can feel like the end, but it doesn't have to be. It can actually be the beginning!

it can sometimes appear unbelievable. He exchanges *His beauty* for *our ashes*. He restores what we so easily discard, bringing value to things we have deemed worthless. It was said of Jesus' hometown, "Can anything good come out of Nazareth?"—it was an unlikely place for a Savior to be raised. But Jesus was the tender root that sprang up out of dry ground—an unlikely place for a tender plant to grow. One of the greatest paradoxes is the way His death on the cross brings life to the world. It was said that His crucifixion was so gruesome that people were aghast—unable to even look upon Him. Now we *fix our eyes on Jesus*! He is the desired of nations. Previously lifted up on a cross, impaled as a common criminal, He now draws all people to Himself. He has worldwide magnetism. The stone once rejected is now the Chief Cornerstone.

He truly does work all things together to accomplish His purposes in us. Things we believe will *destroy* us, He fully implements to *transform* us, causing us to *see more* of Jesus and *become more* like Him (Romans 8:28,29). God does not waste one of our trials. Rather, He uses them to prepare us to fulfill our destiny. He is far from indifferent when we go through difficulty. He completely empathizes with us, fully experiencing what we experience. He is a Wonderful Counselor and the deeply compassionate Shepherd of our souls. But He is also an amazing Redeemer, able to maximize whatever life throws at us. *Disappointments* cannot keep Him from fulfilling *His appointments* for us.

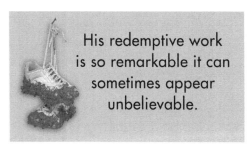

His redemptive work is so remarkable it can sometimes appear unbelievable.

Take Joseph, for example. His brothers' seething jealousy resulted in Joseph being sold as a slave, eventually landing him in Egypt. Injustices abounded for him as a young stranger in a foreign land. Yet in the midst of countless disappointments, Joseph learned valuable lessons in leadership, gaining him favor with

Pharaoh. So much so, that he was lifted from the position of a common slave to becoming one of the highest-ranking rulers in all of Egypt. His most *painful* moments became the pathway to his

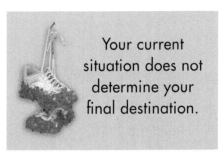

Your current situation does not determine your final destination.

most *purposeful* moment — the saving of Egypt and many other nations in a time of famine. Joseph even rescued his father, Israel, and all of his brothers—the very ones who had betrayed him. His final statement to his brothers reveals the power of living "unstuck." Despite their intentional cruelty, he was able to say to them,

"You intended to harm me, but God intended it for good to accomplish what is now being done, the saving of many lives" (Genesis 50:20).

Your current situation does not determine your final destination. The God who works all things together for good is at work in you! Difficulties don't deter Him. He is the all-terrain Father who is able to accomplish *His best* even when the world gives us *its worst*!

Receive this liberating perspective from James, the half brother of Jesus,

"Count it all joy, my brothers, when you meet trials of various kinds, for you know that the testing of your faith produces steadfastness. And let steadfastness have its full effect, that you may be perfect and complete, lacking in nothing" (James 1:2-4 ESV).

When our faith is tested, we have a choice to make. We can allow disappointment to have its full effect, leading us to despair and unbelief. Or we can let steadfastness have its full effect, causing our trust to deepen and our strength to increase. We will be made perfect. Rather than referring to a life free from mistakes, being "perfect" signifies maturity — exchanging childish tantrums for confident triumphs. Instead of steeping in the confusing thoughts and emotions fueled by discouragement, we learn to live beyond disappointment. In that place, we lack nothing. We have no shortage of faith. Our love is bold and our peace is settled, despite unsettling circumstances. An abundance of wisdom fills us with a perspective that sees beyond the moment. As we trust our Father, His comfort becomes a tangible experience. The God of all comfort will "come fortify" us in all our afflictions, and His strength becomes ours.

I recently returned from a friend's funeral. We are saddened by her departure and are grieving for her husband and family, who will miss her most. But we will not spend the rest of our lives in grief. Solomon wisely said, "There is a time to weep and a time to laugh, a time to mourn and a time to dance" (Ecclesiastes 3:4). People stuck in disappointment spend their entire lives grieving, lamenting what was and what wasn't. What could be and what may never be. But grieving was never intended to become our constant condition. Mourning has a time—a time when

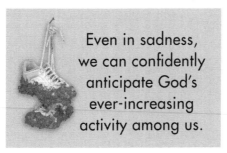

Even in sadness, we can confidently anticipate God's ever-increasing activity among us.

it is the compassionate response to an immediate sadness. Yet it is a time—one having a starting point and an ending point. And even when we do grieve, we do not grieve "as those who have no hope" (1 Thessalonians 4:13). Even in sadness, we can confidently anticipate God's ever-increasing activity among us.

My friend died, but her inspiration lives on. She is resting with our Father in the heavenly realms, while the fruit of her life here on earth continues to grow. She prayed for lots of people; lost ones, found ones, broken ones, healing ones. Not all of her prayers were answered while she was on the earth, but God is still actively fulfilling the cries of her heart. Many more people will be restored to their Father simply because she prayed and never gave up. Our cooperative ventures with the Lord are *never* in vain.

Consider Abram, who navigated life with a name meaning "exalted father," although he had no children. Then the Lord upgraded him to Abraham, "father of multitudes"…and still he had not received his promised son. Probably starting in his 20s and continuing right through his 90s, he had ample opportunities to feel the sting of disappointment. How he must have longed to hold a baby close to his heart, hear childish chatter in his tent, and pour all his wisdom into an heir. For eighty years he lived with perplexity, yet chose to see God as his friend.

Imagine if Abraham's desire had been established, in the way he likely "thought" it should have

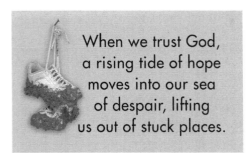

When we trust God, a rising tide of hope moves into our sea of despair, lifting us out of stuck places.

unfolded. He would have been the proud father of a hearty family, with perhaps a dozen children and one hundred grandkids to rock on his knees. Yet ultimately Abraham inherited something infinitely greater than being blessed by and a blessing to his earthly family. In God's economy of honor and increase, he additionally became the father through whom *"all families on earth will be blessed"* (Gen 12:3 NLT).

Many people become like boats stuck on a sandbar, unable to move forward because they're disappointed with past events. In the words of Paul, they have "shipwrecked their faith" (1 Timothy 1:19). But when we trust God and look to Him as the friend who is supporting us and planning to redeem every painful place, a rising tide of hope moves into our sea of despair, lifting us out of stuck places. No longer sidelined, we take courageous risks once more, and become reenergized warriors who will restore many others to the place of renewed faith.

Yes, there is a life ahead that supersedes today's disappointment. It's a place of revived hope. And it's *your* place. God said to His people, Israel, after they had been wandering in the wilderness for forty years on their way to the Promised Land, "You've been going around in circles in these hills long enough; go north" (Deuteronomy 2:3 MSG).

He says to *you* in *your* wilderness, "You've been going around in circles long enough. Follow Me. Let Me take you to a new place with Me." You are not a victim. You have a choice. There is a place for you, a path to get there, and promises to inherit. He is drawing you closer. Follow Him, and you will *not* be disappointed!

To order more copies of

HOPE

Beyond Disappointment

please go to:

https://www.createspace.com/4431611